TO DIE WITH STYLE!

TO DIE WITH STYLE!

Marjorie Casebier McCoy

Nashville ● ABINGDON PRESS ● New York

TO DIE WITH STYLE!

Library of Congress Cataloging in Publication Data

MCCOY, MARJORIE CASEBIER, 1934-
   To die with style!
   Bibliography: p.
   1. Death—Psychology. I. Title.
BF789.D4M3   155.9'37   74-10573

ISBN 0-687-42199-3

Scripture quotations are from the Revised Standard Version of the Bible, copyrighted 1946, 1952, and 1971, by the Division of Christian Education, National Council of Churches, and are used by permission.

"Question" (copyright 1954 May Swenson) is reprinted by permission of Charles Scribner's Sons from To Mix with Time by May Swenson.

The Living Will, pp. 30-31, is used with permission of the Euthanasia Educational Council.

"when god lets my body be" copyright, 1923, 1951, by E. E. Cummings. Reprinted from his volume, Complete Poems 1913-1962, by permission of Harcourt Brace Jovanovich, Inc. (1972), and MacGibbon & Kee (1968).

The poem "Upon Arriving at 50," by Elizabeth G. Berryhill, is used with her permission.

The quotation from Slow Dance on the Killing Ground, by William Hanley, is © Copyright, as an unpublished work, 1964, by William Hanley. © Copyright, 1964, by William Hanley. Used by permission of the publisher, Random House, Inc.

"Do not go gentle into that good night," from The Poems of Dylan Thomas, copyright 1952 by Dylan Thomas. Reprinted by permission of New Directions Publishing Corporation, J. M. Dent & Sons Ltd., and the Trustees for the Copyrights of the late Dylan Thomas.

Lines on p. 86 reprinted by permission of William Morrow & Co., Inc., from Lost in the Stars by Maxwell Anderson. Copyright © 1949 by Maxwell An-

MANUFACTURED BY THE PARTHENON PRESS AT
NASHVILLE, TENNESSEE, UNITED STATES OF AMERICA

For my nephew,
Mark Heether-Blevins
(1954–1973),

and for
my mother,
my father,
my grandparents,
James West,
Ella Patz,
James Berryhill,
Helen Heilman,
Helen Berryhill,
and Lutie McCoy,
who have achieved their deaths.

"There is a land of the living
and a land of the dead
and the bridge is love . . ."

Thornton Wilder,
The Bridge of San Luis Rey

CONTENTS

ACKNOWLEDGMENTS

This book has been gestating within me for a long, long time. I cannot hope to acknowledge all the sources contributing to its growth and development, but I must mention some of them.

I think of the people to whom I dedicate these pages. In their living and in their dying they touched my life in its deepest places. I knew them and loved them, and because they have died I know I can die also, and die with a little less fear and trembling. They have gone before me like explorers into the unknown, each cutting the path a little wider and a little clearer for me to see. I have never been a Christopher Columbus or a Daniel Boone. As I die I will cling to the knowledge they have gone ahead into strange territory and I will follow their footprints with gratitude.

I think of all the teachers and professors who have helped me understand my own thoughts and experiences, and of my friends and colleagues who have encouraged me to express them.

I think particularly of Dr. Robert Lee, believing in me and urging me to take the risk of writing. Indeed, this work grows out of the book he and I wrote together—*The Spouse Gap: Weathering the Marriage Crisis During Middlescence*. When we were developing the section on what couples might expect after the middle-age crisis I found a passage by Esther Harding in which she quoted Carl Jung's phrase "the *achievement* of death." This perception of death as achievement exploded in me like a skyrocket and started me on the way toward articulating my own thoughts.

I think of Elizabeth Berryhill, my close friend and colleague in Festival Theatre over the years. We have shared the experience of death as well as of life many times. Elizabeth and our choreographer-friend Jeannde Herst inspired my first total vision of the form for this book as we explored together our individual artistic works-in-progress. I am grateful to both of them for that initial breakthrough, and to Elizabeth for her helpful reactions to the manuscript in its various stages.

I think of Rosalie Moore Brown, Dr. Robert Leslie, and Dr. Harland Hogue who read the Working Prospectus and made helpful suggestions.

And I think especially of my husband, Charles S. McCoy, ever-loving, ever-patient, ever-present to me as I've gone up and down in the writing process. His help in the final editing of the manuscript has been invaluable. It seems strange in a way that this book should finally take shape in the two years since we started our new phase of life together. But perhaps it has only been possible for me to look straight at death from within the joyous covenant we share—working back to back, loving face to face, living side by side.

Marjorie Casebier McCoy
Berkeley, California

INTRODUCTION

Once upon a time there was a little girl who woke up in the middle of the night terrified. Her heart raced. Her ears pounded. Her eyes burned. The dark was alive with the sea roar of silence and the blinking pulsations of blackness. She was feeling what it would be like to die and not to be anymore. She could imagine life going on without her and her not even knowing it was going on without her, and she felt she could not bear it.

She gasped. She wanted to run, to call out, but was imprisoned by the darkness. Then she began to cry. Her mother came into the room and turned on the light. She put her arms around the little girl and held her. "What happened? What's wrong, honey?" The little girl finally described her terror: "I don't want to die and not be." Her mother held her tighter in her arms and rocked her back and forth. "You won't have to worry about that for a *long time!*"

I was that little girl. How I happened to have that experience at that time and in that place I do not know. I only know I have worried about dying and not being ever since.

If I think about my own "not being" very long my breath still gets short, my ears roar, my eyes burn, and

I look wildly about to see if anyone else feels it too. Then I force myself to think about something else. I think about what I'll have for dinner, or the projects I must work on, or a friend I want to call, or the fact that I don't have to worry about dying for a long time yet.

But time left for worrying grows shorter. My mother, whose embrace that night held death and nonbeing at bay, is gone now—into that very darkness from which she saved me.

Existential anxiety is real for me. My feelings of terror at the thought of death are enormous. Still I know this fear is not the whole truth of my experience. There are many times when I can think of death and not be frightened. Usually this is possible when I talk with others about dying—our feelings, fears, questions. Or when I think about dying in terms of the mystery that is life as well as death, affirming both as part of God's creative love for us. Or when I focus on the experience of death as happening within the familiar routines of living.

I know that dying is a real, intrinsic part of life. Why then, I ask myself, should it seem so terribly frightening? The very fact we all must die is in itself an assurance that death is part of the natural rhythm of creation. Must it really be so hard for us to accept? Is dying really foreign to the human impulse to live? Is there a way to live our death—that is, to be alive into the experience of death itself, living while we are dying?

This book grows out of my wrestling with these questions. Reflecting on my own experiences and those of others, I have come to believe it is possible for us to live into our deaths with energy and integrity. It may not be possible to eliminate entirely the existential fear of that awesome Unknown, but I do believe we can consciously utilize the kind of trust and courage with which we face the many unknowns of life. Although we cannot choose never to die, we *can* make choices about *how* we die, and we can choose to die with our own style.

It is encouraging to note the growing interest in talking openly about death and dying. Studies of people with terminal illness, such as the one by Elisabeth Kübler-Ross, show that most people who are dying want to talk about death. Courses offered in high schools and colleges on the subject are swamped with students. Conferences on death and dying draw huge crowds, the general public as well as professional workers.

Those of us attending such courses have even found we are able to laugh at some of our fearful expectations. One class I was in took a field trip to a local mortuary where the director explained their services and took us on a tour of the facilities. It was with some hesitation that many of us entered the embalming room. In silence, eyes wide, we listened and looked as he described the process of embalming and the equipment required. Then he asked for questions. One girl pointed to the corner and, in a hushed voice, inquired, "What is *that* used for?" We all turned and saw a gleaming, chrome-plated box with dials and a huge funnel-shaped cone extending from the side. Our imaginations whirled nervously. The director smiled. "That," he said, "is a hair dryer!" Everyone laughed and relaxed. The embalming room suddenly had been given a more natural and human dimension.

Author-teacher Max Steele has been quoted as saying he believes death will succeed pornography as the next, and perhaps final, obscenity. Certainly it is true that until recently in our culture death has been as much of a taboo subject as sex. But death is not obscene. This interest in the part of living we call dying seems to me both healthy and exciting.

Reflecting the growing interest in death and dying are the many books and articles that have appeared. Literature is available that analyzes general cultural attitudes toward death, speculates on the mystery and meaning of death, describes the dying process, or discusses related subjects such as grief, suicide, old age, ethical dilemmas, ministering to the dying, and so forth.

My intention has emerged from this new interest in death, but at the same time I have sought a different, more radically positive way to view dying. I propose we look at death not primarily as a thing to be suffered but rather as an action to be anticipated and prepared for. Dying need not be equated with a watch running down or a flower withering away, as a stream drying up or a rock falling at last into a dark abyss. Why not, with Carl Jung, speak of "the *achievement* of death" and view dying as the final creative task of our lives?

I want to carry forward this notion of death as achievement by exploring some of the possible ways we can take a vital, positive part in shaping how we die. If we can awaken our imagination to envision our own death, then just maybe we can make certain choices about the kind of death we die. I believe such an endeavor will be a force in our living as well as our dying. If the imagination is opened up and the will engaged in the achieving of our own death, is it not likely we will be summoned also to reflect on the style of life we want to live for which that style of death becomes an appropriate extension?

In saying this I am not suggesting there is an "ideal" way to die. While Christian faith is a very important part of my own personal life, I do not believe there is a single Christian style of dying into which we should try to force people, as into an alien, Procrustean bed. There is the reality of Christian faith about death and resurrection which undergirds our living and dying. There is also, for many, the continual struggle of being and becoming Christians who die at different stages in their own growth and understanding. And there is a variety of faiths, each with diverse styles of living. It is impossible to speak of *the* ideal way to live or die.

Those who work with dying patients say over and over again that most people die the way they have lived: pessimists die pessimistically, optimists die optimistically, the selfish die selfishly, the generous die generously. I am inclined to believe that the impending crisis of death can be an occasion for change, if a person's heart is not too filled with fear or too resistant to change, or if the physical and mental processes are not so ravaged that the individual has no residual ability for self-control.

However, the immediate presence of approaching death certainly is no time for "shoulds" and "oughts" about how to die. Death is the time above all when we must be most deeply personal, tying together the threads of all our days into our final achievement. This is the time when we must be allowed to be most really ourselves, for better or worse, hard as this may be on family and friends, doctors and nurses. Each of us needs to be given "room" to die.

Most important, I think, the observation that we die the way we live shows us the need for self-awareness. The earlier we become conscious of our life styles (and thus our potential death styles) the more freedom we will have to change our attitudes, to grow in maturity, to make appropriate decisions, to achieve our death throughout our living.

So let us not wait until we have been hit by a car or

by a terminal illness to look at ourselves in our living and dying. Events may confront us abruptly with the necessity that we come to terms with how we feel about death. But now we can begin to help one another toward heightened awareness in living. We can break through the taboo surrounding death. With the help of the experience of others we can extend our vision and consider dying as a real part of our living. With the help of experience mirrored in literature we can expand our powers of imagination for dying and perhaps learn what it means not only to live but also to die—with style!

I
AWARENESS

To learn to live and to learn how to die are one and the same thing.

Karl Jaspers

BEGINNING REFLECTIONS: TO BE OR NOT TO BE?

To be, or not to be: that is the question:
Whether 'tis nobler in the mind to suffer
The slings and arrows of outrageous fortune,
Or to take arms against a sea of troubles,
And by opposing end them? To die: to sleep;
No more; and, by a sleep to say we end
The heart-ache and the thousand natural shocks
That flesh is heir to, 'tis a consummation
Devoutly to be wish'd. To die, to sleep;
To sleep: perchance to dream: ay, there's the rub;
For in that sleep of death what dreams may come
When we have shuffled off this mortal coil,
Must give us pause. . . .

. . . Who would fardels bear,
To grunt and sweat under a weary life,
But that the dread of something after death,
The undiscover'd country from whose bourn
No traveller returns, puzzles the will,

And makes us rather bear those ills we have
Than fly to others that we know not of?

[*Hamlet,* Act III, Scene I]

Here is Hamlet's familiar question. In the soliloquy we see at once a young man's inner struggle over whether or not to kill himself. At one time or another most of us probably entertain such thoughts. Sometimes in exasperation we may toy with the idea of suicide as escape. Occasionally we may seriously wrestle with suicide as an end to pain and intolerable suffering.

But Hamlet's question pushes us to consider the deeper implications of such action. In Shakespeare's cosmic mirror we are brought face to face with the meaning of "being" and "nonbeing." Hamlet's own image of being is clearly reflected, but the image of nonbeing has the shape of a big question mark. He projects a vision of something worse than the worst of life, but realizes that anything he imagines is distorted because he does not know what lies beyond death.

This dimension of Hamlet's question also touches most of us. For is it not the dreadful frustration at not knowing the content of death which plagues us in those "three-o'clock-in-the-morning" times when we stare into the night sweating and wide-eyed?

DEATH ANXIETY

The anxiety, the fear, the *Angst* of death is real for everyone. Some recognize the experience at an early age and spend their whole lives wondering about the meaning of life and death. Others attempt to repress their feelings, only to have them re-surface at later times in their lives. Sooner or later we confront the fact that finitude is not a coat we can take off and leave behind us; it is the very shape of our humanity. Like children afraid of the dark we regard the unknown of death with fear and trembling. But whereas the dark is simply the dark, death may be nonbeing.

When I first started working on this book a teen-age daughter said to me one day, "I've been meaning to ask you. What *do* you think about death? Are you looking *forward* to it, or what?" I wanted to say something terribly noble and inspiring. Instead I answered, "No, I don't look forward to death. I'm afraid of it." She nodded and smiled at me. "Yeah, like everybody else!"

Like everybody else. The dread of death is shared by others. Knowing that, I feel less alone and less afraid. But I need to be reminded of it over and over. Our shared anxiety is not so obvious when I am lost in the depths of my own self.

Some may try to overcome the anxiety of death with far-out suggestions and pseudo-scientific speculations: "Arrange to have yourself frozen at death and then be thawed out later to live again!" "Anti-aging pills will keep your cells rejuvenating themselves so you can live forever!" Science is experimenting with ways to prolong life, but there are no serious studies that show death on its way out. Those of us living today know we are mortal and will die.

As long as death is abstract and seemingly distant from us we can usually handle it all right. Of course people die; it's the way things are. But when death becomes personal, when *my* mother, *my* father, *my* son die, when I remember that I die, it is a different matter. In the preface to *Three Plays,* Thornton Wilder articulates this sense of the particular character of human experience for us: "'I love you,' 'I rejoice,' 'I suffer,' have been said and felt many billions of times, and never twice the same." I experience my own uniqueness. The source of my life rests in me, and when I die life as I have known it will cease to be for me. No wonder the thought of particular, personal death makes me anxious.

THE WILL TO LIVE

A good part of our death anxiety is the fault of nature itself, which gives us an instinct for survival in a constantly threatening world. Had the human spirit not been created with an innate will to live we might never have survived as a species. The reflex that makes us jump out of the way of a speeding car has kept many of us alive longer than might otherwise have been the case. So there is a sense in which we fight our own natures in seeking to conquer our fear of death.

But we know also that there is a given limit to the life span for every person. Humans are probably the only creatures aware of their own inevitable death. There is for each of us a "deadline," a final point in time, from which no reflex, skill, or insight ultimately can save us. It is easy to see why fear of death is a normal, healthy reaction. It is less clear why we do not have a similar instinct to help us accept our own natural, innate, and inevitable death.

Many of us have a strong conviction that there is something about the self, the "I," that does not die when the body dies. Strong religious belief may be a key factor in reducing death anxiety, reassuring the believer that something of the self lives on. But religious faith is no guarantee of immunity against anxiety in the presence of Hamlet's question. The great religions of the world have long been concerned with issues of human meaning, time, and death. Adherents of a religious belief need not feel guilty when they struggle with these questions. To feel fear in the face of death and nonbeing is natural, for the faithful as for anyone else.

We can say "yes" to belief in a God who created this life and will create a different one for us when this one ends, and still feel the dread of losing the self as we know it in earthly form. May Swenson expresses this uncertainty for us in her poem "Question":

Body my house
my horse my hound
what will I do
when you are fallen

Where will I sleep
How will I ride
What will I hunt

Where can I go
without my mount
all eager and quick
How will I know
in thicket ahead
is danger or treasure
when Body my good
bright dog is dead

How will it be
to lie in the sky
without roof or door
and wind for an eye

With cloud for shift
how will I hide?

For all their problems and limitations, their aches and pains, our bodies are still familiar and comfortable. We hate for them to grow old and die—indeed, we can scarcely imagine ourselves without them!

Logically we might think people with the most love

for life and their bodies would be most afraid of losing them in death. And, conversely, people who are disillusioned with life and loathe their bodies would welcome death as an end to misery. But experience usually reveals the opposite. People who have led satisfying and meaningful lives seem most able to accept death, whereas those who have been unable to enjoy life often continue clinging to it with greatest tenacity.

Perhaps the key to overcoming fear of death rests somehow in the love of life itself and in our instinct for survival. If I embrace my inherent will to live and love life as it is, then I can also embrace the natural fact of death as part of my life. My fear of dying is lessened by loving and trusting the life that contains death. *Because* I love my life and my body I can accept my death—for loving life all the way enables me to die for that love.

SUICIDE

There are times, we know, when the will to live weakens. During periods of severe depression, pain, despair, anxiety, almost everyone has considered Hamlet's question, "To be or not to be," in its literal sense. Most of us choose rather to "bear those ills we have than fly to others that we know not of." Yet a large number of people do take their own lives. Indeed, suicide in the United States now ranks among the top ten killers. How do we explain this action in the light of our basic human fear of death?

Human beings are complex systems of interacting parts. While the physical organism affects the psychological processes, the reverse is true also. A strong and pervasive loss of meaning for a person can cause the repression or even destruction of the life instinct. When we lose the strength and reason for

26

living it is understandable that our impulse toward survival might weaken and the fear of death be dulled.

It is not necessarily true, however, that the suicidal person faces dying unafraid. A neurotic fear of death can draw a person toward that which is feared and thus precipitate the act of suicide. Or, as the French psychotherapist Ignace Lepp has observed, in his book *Death and Its Mysteries,* people with suicidal tendencies may be terrified of death, "but they are even more afraid of the trials and responsibilities of life." Problems that ordinarily could be met and handled may suddenly seem terrifying and insoluble; suicide appears to be the only positive act possible.

Those who work with suicidal people have discovered that, for the most part, people who take their own lives are operating in a tight, constricted frame of mind. The options for choice and action seem severely limited. No resources are apparent to them, only the overwhelming, immediate problems at hand. Seeing no further than the frustration, the guilt, the rage, or the hate that has led them to the moment of self-destruction, suicide becomes a kind of simultaneous revenge on others and punishment of the self.

It is questionable whether people bent on suicide can really consider Hamlet's question in all its dimensions. "To be or not to be" is not their issue, but rather getting back at the world or at some person, or simply giving up that which has lost its meaning. If they could really imagine the consequences of their actions, the absolute finality of their own death, or if they could break out of the constricted mind-set in order to visualize possible alternatives, it is unlikely they would take their own lives.

Albert Camus has called suicide the "one truly serious philosophical problem." In his long essay

27

"The Myth of Sisyphus," he laboriously works out his own argument against suicide. For him the world is irrational and death is the final absurdity. Seeing this fact with clarity, he believes, frees us to accept our existence and to live our fate with defiance. Taking one's own life, for Camus, would be to yield to the absurdity. Thus Camus's Sisyphus, condemned to roll his huge stone back to the top of the mountain (from which it rolls back down) forever, finds a kind of strange happiness in defiantly accepting and embracing his destiny and suffering.

I mention this view because I believe it is an articulate and sensitive attempt to deal with the question of suicide. Many have found in Camus a helpful rationale for courage to live and act in a world perceived to be indifferent at best and demonic at worst. My own experience of faith leads me to an opposite view. I believe the world wishes me not ill but good. My choice to live is my faithful response to that good intention.

As I look back on my life I can see what I would have missed if I had ever chosen suicide. There have been dark, anxious times. But out of those difficulties I have grown and changed, I have found the fulfillment of significant work, I have known the joy of loving and being loved. In the face of inevitable death I stand with Camus in arguing against suicide—but for quite different reasons.

THE RIGHT TO DIE

We have looked at suicide as a negative response to meaninglessness. Now it is necessary to look at the issue of a person's right to die when one *is* fully aware of the consequences of one's actions and has *not* lost a belief in life's value. Here we might think of Socrates drinking the hemlock, or someone with a terminal illness taking an overdose of sleeping pills, or people giving their lives for causes or for other people. These actions are very different in quality and intent from those we usually associate with suicide. These people, operating within their own personal circumstances, are attempting to exercise some control over the quality of their living and dying.

Death comes to us all eventually. But there may be things in life worse than death. I can imagine that persons with terminal illnesses might take their own lives because they feel living with unremitting pain, agony, and indignity to be worse than dying. I can also imagine that persons in circumstances demanding radical action of life-and-death proportions believe denying their faith and integrity to be worse than dying. They may not will to die, but they do will to live out their loyalties and commitments to whatever conclusions these may lead—even death.

In these instances the question of the right to die becomes an extension of the will to live. It is not that life no longer has meaning; it is precisely because life still has meaning that one may choose to let it go. Those who live with dignity will also want to die with dignity. To be consciously aware of alternatives and then to choose to give up one's life is to take an active part in achieving death in one's own appropriate style.

Whether or not people with terminal illness should have the right to participate in determining their own death has become ambiguous in this time of vastly improved medical care. People used to die at home. In that context the process of dying was understandably simpler. If people couldn't or wouldn't eat, if they refused medication or took too much, if secondary complications hastened the dying, there was an acceptance of these events. Today, however, some 80

29

percent of Americans die in institutions. Under the rigorous supervision of professional care there is little the patient can do. There are ways to feed people who can't or won't eat. Just the right amount of medication is provided and given by whatever means necessary. Secondary complications, infections, pneumonia, side effects are discovered and treated.

This is not to say medical care is undesirable! If I were seriously ill I would go into a hospital immediately. But we do not have much control over ourselves once we are in the care of modern medical technology. The question may finally become one of whether we are really prolonging living or only lengthening the process of dying.

This is essentially the argument used by proponents of euthanasia—a word derived from the Greek, meaning "a good death." The Euthanasia Educational Council, devoted to establishing "the right to die with dignity," has been growing steadily and is deluged with requests for copies of a document it produced called "A Living Will." Addressed to one's family, physician, clergyman, and lawyer, this Will is intended to become effective at any time the person can no longer make decisions for his or her own future. It reads:

Death is as much a reality as birth, growth, maturity and old age—it is the one certainty of life. If the time comes when I, ——— can no longer take part in decisions for my own future, let this statement stand as an expression of my wishes, while I am still of sound mind.

If the situation should arise in which there is no reasonable expectation of my recovery from physical or mental disability, I request that I be allowed to die and not be kept alive by artificial means or "heroic measures". I do not fear death itself as much as the indignities of deterioration, dependence and hopeless pain. I, therefore, ask that medication

30

be mercifully administered to me to alleviate suffering even though this may hasten the moment of death.

This request is made after careful consideration. I hope you who care for me will feel morally bound to follow its mandate. I recognize that this appears to place a heavy responsibility upon you, but it is with the intention of relieving you of such responsibility and of placing it upon myself in accordance with my strong convictions, that this statement is made.

There are people who are afraid this kind of document will open the way for indiscriminate killing of old and sick people, or be a justification for not doing everything possible to help someone terminally ill. A careful reading of this Will and of other literature on euthanasia should make clear that it is a person's own right to decide about his or her own death which is being advocated. This is not to be confused with "mercy killing." Here the concern is not killing people, but letting a person die when that individual says "Enough!"

Inherent in Hamlet's question is the option "not to be." The freedom to make such a choice is essential to our full human experience. At the very least, it seems to me, people should be able to refuse "heroic measures" to keep themselves alive. Mrs. Henry J. Mali, President of the Euthanasia Council, expresses her own view this way: "Now that I'm old, the next celebration is death. And what I'm most interested in is how my death can be made an honorable estate, like matrimony" (quoted by Judy Klemesrud in *The New York Times,* March 1, 1971).

DEATH REALITY

Despite growing interest in some circles to discuss death and one's right to die with dignity, there is still a

31

great deal of reluctance among many people to talk about this fact of life. Indicative, I think, was Pablo Picasso's refusal to permit any discussion of death whatsoever in his presence. He was so superstitious about death he refused to make out a will, thus leaving behind him all sorts of chaos relating to inheritance among his legitimate and illegitimate heirs.

Some say our culture today is "death-denying," and cite our preoccupation with youth, our homes for old people to die in, our emphasis on cosmetics for both the living and the dead, the view that talking about death is more taboo than talking about sex. Others describe us as "death-haunted," and point to the way the nuclear bomb hangs over us a threat of life-extinction, and the way the environmental crisis is causing alarm about future resources and the balance of nature. Still others suggest we are "death-preoccupied," and call attention to the violence shown in our movies and on T.V., and to the atrocities of wars abroad and the murders and assassinations at home.

I am inclined to believe each of these views is partially true, and elements of all three can be seen in our society today. Taken together they reflect a conspiracy to distort death: covering it with cosmetics, veiling it with the cosmos, shrouding it with carnage. Like Pablo Picasso we secretly hope that if we do not confront death directly we will never have to face it personally. But even if we live to be ninety-one, as Picasso did, we still die. Unless we come to terms with the reality of death, it is unlikely we will discover the depths of our own resources for either death or life. And our dying will indeed be a lonely affair if we cannot talk about it even with those we love.

How, then, can we discover the way to live into our own death with energy and with our own appropriate style? Certainly the place to begin is with the recognition that living and dying are two sides of the same coin and mutually affect each other. This notion has a good deal of precedent in human thought, and I think it is helpful to look at some of the ways others have articulated this feeling.

Theologian Paul Tillich observes that most of us think only of the immediate future without considering the end of our lives: "Perhaps we could not live without doing so most of our time. But perhaps we will not be able to die if we *always* do so. And if one is not able to die, is he really able to live?"[1] Lewis Mumford is even more specific about what he believes is lost when the fact of death is not taken into consideration: "When vitality runs high, death takes men by surprise. But if they close their eyes to this possibility, what they gain in peace they lose in sensibility and significance; and not least, they then leave themselves unarmed for more serious encounters and more dire defeats."[2] Finally, existentialist philosopher Karl Jaspers ties the two sides of the coin together even more completely: "If to philosophize is to learn how to die, then this learning how to die is actually the condition for the good life. To learn to live and to learn how to die are one and the same thing."[3]

These men are not talking about a morbid preoccupation with death and dying, and neither am I. To brood about decay and nothingness is to turn away from life and its possibilities for growth, vitality, and love. Such a barren, fruitless existence would very likely end in madness. But shutting out any conscious engagement with the reality of death can rob our lives

[1] "The Eternal Now," in *The Meaning of Death,* ed. Herman Feifel (New York: McGraw-Hill, 1959), p. 32.

[2] *The Conduct of Life* (New York: Harcourt, Brace and Co., 1951), p. 81.

[3] As quoted in Jacques Choron, *Death and Western Thought* (New York: Collier Books, 1963), p. 228.

of deep and significant feeling. Never to wrestle with Hamlet's question is to risk never understanding the wonder and glory and preciousness of this one and only life. "To be," as a whole, individual, unique person, is to live with some knowledge that "not to be" is also part of the fullness of selfhood.

Just as there is no life without death, so too there is no death without life. That is, death was not always around. It arose with life, and its story is dependent on life's story. In saying "yes" to living we must also say "yes" to the dying that is part of life.

LIVING AND DYING IN LIFE

I have no hope. I expect to die while the war continues. But that does not discourage me about making an effort. To do otherwise would be to die in life, and that is what I lament in others. [Letter from a middle-aged Virginia housewife, quoted by Wayne Cowan, *Christianity and Crisis,* October 2, 1972]

Looking at life in its wholeness we know that all of us are born to die. Since death arises with life, there is a sense in which we are dying all of our lives. But just as there are many different ways of living, so too there are many different ways of dying in life before we cease walking around and breathing. This "middle-aged Virginia housewife" knew the difference between these experiences. She was physically dying of cancer; yet she was more alive to a sense of social responsibility than many people around her.

We usually take our livingness for granted, a fact that tends to dull the vitality of our aliveness. Most of us are familiar with the children's bedtime prayer that goes, "Now I lay me down to sleep; I pray the Lord my soul to keep. If I should die before I wake, I pray the

Lord my soul to take." This is a fearful prayer to teach our children, I think, since it suggests they may die if they go to sleep. Perhaps it is a better prayer for us adults who are in danger of sleeping through life, who are likely to "die before we wake" to all the possibilities of being alive.

The threat of illness or accident sometimes jars us awake. When, through experience or imagination, we face the reality of our own death all our experiences become richer. Abraham Maslow writes of his perception as he recuperated from a heart attack:

The confrontation with death—and the reprieve from it —makes everything look so precious, so sacred, so beautiful that I feel more strongly than ever the impulse to love it, to embrace it, and to let myself be overwhelmed by it. My river has never looked so beautiful. . . . Death, and its ever present possibility makes love, passionate love, more possible. I wonder if we could love passionately, if ecstasy would be possible at all, if we knew we'd never die. [Quoted by Rollo May, *Love and Will* (New York: W. W. Norton, 1969), p. 99]

In his novel *The Ides of March,* Thornton Wilder imagines a similar understanding for his central character, Julius Caesar: "Only those who have grasped their non-being are capable of praising the sunlight. I will have no part in the doctrine of the stoics that the contemplation of death teaches us the vanity of human endeavor and the insubstantiality of life's joys. Each year I say farewell to the spring with a more intense passion" (Signet; New York: New American Library, 1963, p. 144). Our passionate love and commitment rest within our finitude. Only when we recognize the transient quality of the world do we seem to gain a heightened sense of the wonder and richness of life.

DEFINING DYING AND DEATH

There is a difference between the act of dying and the event of death itself. The first is a process filled with various particular experiences of livingness. The second is that moment when the vital functions we call life cease. It is also the "forever after" state of the body of the person who has died.

Some of us are most afraid of the last stages of dying. At the end of her study *On Death and Dying* (New York: Macmillan, 1970), Elisabeth Kübler-Ross observes that among her patients "death itself is not the problem, but dying is feared because of the accompanying sense of hopelessness, helplessness, and isolation." There may be fear also of terrible pain, of suffering the indignities of a failing physical system, or of consciously knowing one is dying and not being able to do anything to stop it. For many who fear the agony of dying the thought of resuscitation or of being hooked to a respirator indefinitely only adds to the fear. They see such practices as perhaps prolonging their suffering needlessly.

For others, death looms as the more fearful and terrifying experience. e. e. cummings begins one of his poems saying: "dying is fine)but Death / ?o / baby."[1] For cummings and others of us it is the stark, cold finality of death that makes us apprehensive. Hard as they are to bear, pain and suffering are at least familiar to us, whereas whatever it is we are after death is strange. Although these people do not want to linger and suffer, they may not want to die suddenly either. Some see the period of dying as their preparation to enter that realm they fear.

On the surface, the difference between dying and

[1]*Complete Poems 1913-1962* (New York: Harcourt Brace Jovanovich, 1972; and London: MacGibbon & Kee, 1968).

death seems obvious. Either a person is breathing, warm, soft; or still, cold, stiff. But the matter is no longer simple. Science has made it possible to keep the heart beating and the lungs breathing by mechanical means long after the body is unable to sustain them. Even when the brain waves have ceased and there is no possibility of recovery, those organs can be kept functioning for some time. In such a case is the body technically alive or dead?

Establishing the precise moment of death thus has become a complex medical and legal issue. The old criteria are now inadequate. Medicine, pushed by the courts, is running to catch up with its own advances by proposing new guidelines to help determine when dying becomes death. It may take considerable time to reach a new technical definition of death. In the meantime, however, for the person who dies, the exact moment of death remains something of a moot point!

WATCHING THE YEARS ACCRUE

We all are dying all the time in that process called aging. Even as growing children we are in motion toward those later years when the body will slow down, the organs wear out, the muscles lose their tone, the skin develop wrinkles, the cells die without replacing themselves. It has been said that the only "cure" for old age is an early death! Improved medical care has reduced the number of early deaths from disease, and better nutrition slows down the aging process. But to live is to go through the biological changes we know as "growing up" and "growing old."

If we are to discover the way to die with style, we must become aware of our own feelings about aging.

We know we must make certain physical adjustments as the years pass. It is necessary to face the gradual transition in appearance—our most visible reminder of our mortality. Even more difficult are the psychological and emotional upheavals of growing old. How we adapt will have consequences for the way we achieve our death. But attitudes in society do not help and may impede our adjustment.

Our time glorifies youth and ignores the elderly. "The young are on their way up, the old are on their way out," is the unspoken feeling. T.V. commercials, fashions, career training, education, job opportunities—all are directed toward young people. Our society emphasizes self-sufficiency and rugged individualism. Old age becomes a shameful, awkward state as waning ability to be independent brings loss of self-esteem and feelings of guilt.

Another factor in the emotional trauma of old age has been the praise of work as the indicator of human worth. Forced to retire, unable to be a "producer" either because of social regulation or declining health, the older person raised on the work ethic loses the central meaning of life.

It is no wonder that older people often die in life long before they die physically—through boredom, emptiness, and futility. If they aren't pushed out by society, they quietly drop out and hibernate in a room somewhere or sit in a convalescent hospital. If this isolation and sense of self-denigration is what we have to look forward to in our later years, we will be hard put to die with life as any kind of vigorous achievement! We must begin now to find new perspective on the later years.

One thing we can do now is look at retirement as a time of transition and genuine life crisis. As such, the retirement years can also be an occasion for shaping new goals and understandings, for re-assessing new life styles and values. To grow old is not a shameful or embarrassing mistake—it is one of the important stages in our process of living. We need such a time for pursuing the desires of our hearts, for enjoying the fruits of our labors, and for wrestling with the ultimate concerns of our lives.

There have been many elderly people who were far from dead in life, people who found meaning and interest in their later years: Picasso painting until a few hours before his death at ninety-one, Bertrand Russell publishing his last book at ninety-one, Verdi composing *Falstaff* at eighty. Mrs. Florida Scott-Maxwell started her training as a psychotherapist at fifty and wrote her memoirs after she was eighty. Lena Mendelson at seventy-eight works as a volunteer helping children learn to read. One great-grandmother started learning Greek at breakfast because that was her only free time!

If we could only relax more into age and enjoy the life in which we grow old we would find many delights and pleasures along the way. I love this "self-centered poem of gratitude to her friends" written by my friend Elizabeth Berryhill on her fiftieth birthday—hardly "old" but reflecting thoughts on the matter of aging:

UPON ARRIVING AT 50

The years accrue
And with them, other realities:
Wrinkles, bulges, gray in the hair,
Strange brown spots on the hands and arms,
Shortness of breath when walking fast,
The book that must be held at arm's length
   to be read,
An image in the mirror of Someone Else

(Surely that's not *Me!*),
Doubt, confusion, anger, fear.

   (Fear . . . !
   The sled is coasting down the hill
     too fast . . . too fast . . . !)

Why, then, roll off it and lie still.
   (Why didn't *I* think of that?
   Here I go-o-o-o-o-o-o!)

Lie still and look and listen.
   (Lie still here in the snow?
   It's cold, it's wet, it hurts!)

Lie still.

Now, is it snow?
   (Why, no. Surprise, surprise!
   It is still earth and warm.)

Yes.
And in the daytime, sun shines overhead
   or rain falls,
And candles can be lit at night, and fires,
And songs are here to sing
And poems to be made,
And friends stand 'round about
   in trust and love.

   (Thank God for friends
     to trust and love.)

Thank God.

Every day there is more of us to be expressed in our relationships and activities, for nothing of us need be lost. Our youth is still present in our age, our accomplished work is present in our rest, our self-sufficiency is present in our acceptance of help. It takes time and experience to grow old. We have every right to wear our years with dignity, and to make our transition into death with *life.*

FACING FATAL ILLNESS

There also are those of us who are dying in life from some specific disease rather than from the inevitable ravages of aging. A terminal illness ends the life span sooner than the natural process. Death, which has lurked somewhere in the distant future, comes sharply into immediate focus. The projected years of one's life must get telescoped somehow into the years, months, or days it takes the disease to do its work.

We might suppose that people who know they have only a short time to live would give up and die to life, letting themselves be carried passively into death. But this is not always the case. More often than not, the terminally ill feel the shortness of time and concentrate on living each day as fully as possible. One man, facing his fatal disease, wrote: "In a way, illness is liberating. It liberates you from all the nonsense that we allow to crowd into our lives. It makes you think more about the quality of life—with what to do with what you've got. When I wake up, I wake up with the feeling, 'let's not waste today'" (quoted by Roy Larson in *San Francisco Sunday Examiner and Chronicle,* April 1, 1973). Rather than less vitality, this man experiences greater vitality in his livingness, a deeper, more intense quality of feeling.

When we imagine the style in which we achieve our own death, we will need to ask ourselves whether we want to be told if we have a terminal illness. I personally think it *is* necessary to know in order to live into my own death. Perhaps I will still go through the times of denial, anger, bargaining, depression, and (I hope!) acceptance—stages Dr. Kübler-Ross describes. But knowing and being prepared may make the stages easier to bear and understand and accept.

At a time when the sham and façade of life are so

futile it would seem terrible to try to live as though nothing were seriously wrong. If relatives know I am dying and don't want me to know they know, and vice versa, energy and time are wasted in mere game-playing. To be able to talk about what means most seems to me very important. It is all right to be sad together, to cry, to mourn; beyond these there is love and caring and presence together. I realize that some people may not want to know they are fatally ill. But now is the time for all of us to explore the implications of knowing and not knowing, and to make those around us aware of our wishes.

It is hard now for me to imagine what it would be like to know I have only a short time to live. As I try to do so, I have great feelings of grief and sadness, observing the poignancy of each little thing I might be doing for the last time. But I know from experience that the "generality" of a thing always comes to us as "particulars." If I knew I would die next month I would still have teeth to brush each morning, cats to feed, my husband to kiss good-bye as he left for the office. In the day-by-day routine of living we are ourselves and become ourselves. That very routine may sustain us in a penultimate way so that we can concentrate our energies on the ultimate task before us.

SUFFERING THE LITTLE DEATHS

Dying in life can be seen also in the experiences of endings, partings, separations, and losses that each of us has over and over. Indeed, if death is the final separation, then each separation and loss in life is a "little death." Graduating from school, changing jobs, moving from one community to another, experiencing the end of a project, as well as defeat, failure, divorce, death of family and friends—all these are precursors of our own death. How we handle these little deaths will have a profound affect on how we come to terms with our own time of dying.

There is something very poignant to me about change. When I was young my family moved a number of times as my father's work location changed. I remember how hard it was for me every time we left some place. "This is where I learned to dance!" "This is where I wrote my first poem!" "This is where I got my bicycle!" "This is where I know people and they know me!" Each time we moved I knew I would never again have such good friends or know such joy. But I did.

It is hard to know whether my own desire for permanence is the result of those early days of impermanence. I do know my experiences of change and the new growth and insight that came from them helped to temper my longing for the changeless with necessary realism. The separations have served as reminders that we are pilgrims in a world of continual change.

How many of us have tried to recapture a certain feeling or event, or have returned to a place we lived or a school we attended, only to find it is not the same as we remember? It is true that "we can't go home again" in the sense that we cannot return to something from which we've moved away. And even if we never move from home we can't return to the past of our childhood, which we know in memory. Each day we are a little different, others are a little different.

We really know that many of our separations and losses are appropriate and necessary. Certain things must be left behind if we are to grow; change is often for our own good, keeping us from stagnating and becoming "dead in life" while still physically alive. Hanging on too long to what once was can distort its true significance in the flow of our lives. In nostalgia we may long to go back to a time when things seemed "sure," forgetting that we were no more sure then than we are now. Part of our search for an appropriate style of life and death involves discovering how and when to "let go."

We must allow ourselves to mourn the passing of such experiences in an appropriate manner. Through the mourning we make our adjustments to the changes, have our private "summing-up" times for important periods of our lives. We must live our separations and not box them away too soon. But rather than letting a piece of ourselves die in the loss we can pick up and contain that loss in a new forward surge of energy.

Next to our own death, the death of someone we love deeply is the hardest separation we must face. We miss all the things that can only come through the physical presence of the other person—the jokes shared, the embraces, the conversation, the interaction, the growing together. In death the person gets frozen to a certain period of time in our lives, and we mourn the lack of opportunity to share the new experiences we are having. In our own death we know we will be separated from all we love and is familiar to us. Life will go on without us, and we won't be part of it.

Lecomte du Noüy suggests in *Human Destiny* that "from an evolutive point of view the greatest invention of Nature is death." We live because others before us have died, and others will have life because we die. This knowledge does not make the sense of loss or separation any easier. It does put death in cosmic perspective, as an intrinsic part of the structure of life.

Humanity itself presses toward the future and carries us along, encouraging us to discard the old mementos that clutter our lives. Holding on to nostalgic remembrances too long binds us to the past and keeps us forever re-dying the same losses and separations. Out of old experiences come new insights, giving us strength to live life deeply and courage to achieve death fully.

THE DARK NIGHT OF THE SOUL

Growing old, terminal illness, separations and changes are all forms of dying in life with which we must contend. When they come, however, they *can* be experiences of life as well as death—occasions by which we are enabled to renew the quality of our own daily living in the presence of death itself.

There is yet another form of dying in life, however, which attacks the very feeling-centers of ourselves and suppresses our ability to hope, to believe, to love. This is the death that is born of despair. It is the depression and hopelessness that erode our spirits and kill us long before our hearts stop beating and our brain waves cease. It is the dark night of meaninglessness, alienating us from all that makes life worth living. It is being dead in life in its most tragic sense.

Despair feeds on itself. It may arise out of a sense of discouragement with the world, disgust with the self, disillusionment with others. These feelings then are compounded by the attendant belief that nothing can change and that time is too short to start anew. Charles Morgan in *The Empty Room* calls despair "a disease, an insomnia of the soul that forbids its own healing."

Jonathan Miller, in an article entitled "The Story of a Death in the City" (*San Francisco Chronicle,* February 15, 1972), wrote of a twenty-three-year-old girl who jumped to her death from the fourth floor of a San Francisco apartment house. The police report indicated she had been on welfare and was on probation after being convicted of visiting a place where drugs were used. She had been arrested once on a drug charge. Reportedly, she had dropped acid and experienced LSD flashbacks. Those facts alone are not unusual today. But behind this report is the story of a young girl from an upper-middle-class family who dropped out of college to come to San Francisco. She had not worked for two years and was living with a young man in a dreary apartment, her fifth apartment in five months. Her companion described her as lonely and confused but couldn't explain why she would want to kill herself. Then he remembered that two hours earlier, at three o'clock on a Sunday morning, they had been out looking for food in trash cans. He commented, "I think that freaked her out." His observation seems accurate. She had experienced a final crushing indignity. The story unfolds as a downward-spiraling sense of despair from which death finally seemed the only escape.

Deep, existential despair is a hard thing to fight. Søren Kierkegaard describes it as the "sickness unto death." The self is tormented by the agony of a living death from which there is no release. Those who emerge from bouts of despair often are able to see some of the severe psychological, emotional, and spiritual problems that fed their depression: unresolved conflicts, overwhelming feelings of inferiority, guilt, and self-hate. But while "the dark night of the soul" encompassed them, the despair was enhanced by the fearful belief they could never escape from it.

What then is to be done when these times of despair bring death into our life? How does the vitality of livingness return? We never know ahead of time how or from where the flash of insight comes to illumine the darkness with hope. If we did, we would not be in despair! Therefore, it seems to me, we can only be as receptive as possible to whatever sources of light may penetrate our particular despair.

We can talk to others—if only about the despair that deadens our desire to talk at all. It is at least a beginning, and the talking may touch on just that thing which brings a breakthrough.

We can do *something*—if only of the most commonplace and ordinary nature. Perhaps a walk in the air, cleaning house, a drive, writing a letter, working in the garden, will be the occasion for receiving the needed stimulus.

We can read something—if only about another person's struggle with despair. Sometimes the recognition that we are not the only ones who are troubled can put us on the way out of our individual sense of hopelessness.

And, if none of these help or are impossible even to do, we can endure the dark night with patience. After all, it is *life* itself that sustains the living death we experience, and life is never entirely static. Perhaps, as Unamuno writes in *Tragic Sense of Life,* "Anguish leads us to consolation."[2] When we feel farthest from God we may indeed be closest. Though in despair we feel most hopeless, it is because we have known hope that we are able to know its absence. And if we had it once it is still there in the recesses of our spirits, waiting to assert itself again through the smallest crack in the blackness.

SEEING THE WHOLENESS

While there are final distinctions to be made between living and dying, and between dying and death, we know they interact throughout our experi-

[2]Trans. J. E. Crawford Flitch (New York: Dover, 1954), p. 57.

ence. If we can be dying or dead in life, is it not possible to be living and alive into our deaths? I think this was true for Elaine, a woman Robert Kavanaugh tells about in his book *Facing Death* (Los Angeles: Nash Publishing, 1972). After describing her fears when she learned of her fatal illness and after living through the months of debilitating sickness, she wrote the following:

> I wish someone had told me that the only impossible fear is the fear to feel and share your feelings with others. Those who love you can understand anything and all of us are stronger than any of us realize. I think my death will be almost happy, since my one pressing regret is that I cannot live to practice what I learned in dying. [P. 57]

Perhaps she did not have long to practice what she had learned, but she certainly was practicing it as she lived into her dying.

The wholeness is there—the rhythm of living and dying present together throughout our lives in dynamic interrelationship. Each has meaning against the background of the other. Sometimes one is primary for us as we look at the meaning of our lives, and sometimes the other is central. With self-awareness we can choose where to focus our attention at any given time so that our living and dying enhance each other.

Rollo May tells of a patient of his who had a terrifying feeling that she was dying while under gas in a dentist's chair. Over and over she kept hearing herself say, "Death is for the living, life is for the dying." This experience radically changed her whole way of looking at her life and her relationships. By reversing what we usually think of as "death for the dying and life for the living" she found a new configuration of meaning. Life was suddenly filled with a sense of preciousness and wonder, difficulties did not loom so large, the new seemed possible, she could assert herself with greater force.

In reflecting on her experience, Dr. May writes:

One of the things it says to me is, death is *for* life, and life is for death. That is, you are reborn into life by dying. This would make it an experience in which she joins the race —an experience celebrated in different cultures by the rite of baptism—dying to be born again. It is also the myth and rite of resurrection—dying to be raised again. [*Power and Innocence* (New York: W. W. Norton, 1972), pp. 92, 93]

This new life is possible for all of us, I think. Each of us dies in life many times before we achieve the final death, and each of those deaths is *for* the life we are living. Though we may be dying all of our lives, the dying feeds the living itself, resurrecting us at each moment into new life: life and death, dying and living, pulsating in the wholeness of our lives.

FINDING OUR STYLES

For almost as long as she has been able to remember, Ruth Hoffman has liked parties.

She liked to give them. She liked to attend them. And for years, as part of a string ensemble, she used to play at them.

Today, between noon and 8:00 P.M., Mrs. Hoffman, 57, will be hostess at what probably will be her last party.

She is dying of cancer and she is having an open house in her room at Sequoia Hospital in Redwood City to bid her family and friends farewell. [*San Francisco Chronicle,* August 11, 1973. © Chronicle Publishing Co., 1973]

I would like to have known Ruth Hoffman. When I read this announcement I felt a great surge of empathy. I could imagine myself in her place and feel the impulse to give a party. Other people, inclined to be more private and withdrawn, might not find this kind of action appropriate, but for Ruth Hoffman it seems just right. It has "style." If we love celebrations in life, then why not celebrate the final achievment also?

The story in the paper the next day reported that

51

Ruth Hoffman's "open house" was a huge success. There were laughter and food and sharing of memories and experiences. The hostess and guest of honor was radiant. I wish I had gone to her party.

I would like to see all of us have the kind of daring and enthusiasm that prompted Ruth Hoffman to host a last party for herself. Certainly the form of the action would be different for each of us, but we would share a kind of basic impulse to express ourselves in our own appropriate ways. I have always been moved by people who die nobly, people who are able to face their death with courage. I think it is because they have become "actors" rather than "victims." They say "yes" to the end of this life with grace and dignity.

Not long ago, as I reflected on how I would like to die, I wrote the following:

When I die I would like:
  to be noble and dignified;
  to have no regrets;
  to have as little pain as possible (I would need a little to help me realize I'm dying!);
  to have people talk to me about dying when I want to;
  to have people (or at least someone) with me so I won't be alone;
  to not be scared;
  to not be embarrassed;
  to be able to laugh;
  to be able to cry.

As I subsequently reread this list I realized it calls for a style that is more straightforward and honest than I am now. By becoming conscious of what I would like to be, however, perhaps I have at least opened the way for growing into the style I imagined.

Ruth Hoffman strikes me as a person who has found her style—in her living and in her dying. I don't know how she did it, but I think it is an important discovery in our journey toward the achievement of our own death.

STYLE AS FORM AND CONTENT

In the artistic realm, style is the way an artist relates the form and the content of his or her work. The artist has something to say or to express and must decide on the way to say or express this meaning in the best way. This giving of an outer shape to the hitherto undefined, undescribed, unarticulated feeling is the art itself.

Within each work of art there is a constant struggle to make the form and content suit each other. I remember a composer saying to a friend of mine, "There are dozens of ways I can set your lyric to music. We just have to be careful that my form doesn't change your meaning."

In life each of us is called to be something of an artist. When I think of the style of an individual life, I see that style as the way a particular person relates the outward form and the inward content of his or her life. In all our relationships and experiences we must try to find the way to best externalize our "me-ness." Whether we call it "trying to find ourselves" or "attempting to get our heads together," we all struggle to express our thoughts and feelings in terms of personally integrated action. Which is to say, we are seeking our own style.

For many of us this style is unconscious and may or may not reflect the wholeness of our inner selves which we would like for others to see. We are all subject to pressures of environment, the accidents of fate, and whatever neurotic difficulties may possess us. The more conscious of these elements we can become, the more freedom we have to make choices about our actions. As human beings we are given certain basic materials from which to shape our lives, but each of us is a uniquely created self continually developing in community with others. The more aware we are of our limitations and possibilities, of our individuality and interdependence, the more likely it is that we will find a style that reflects the content of our whole selves.

Sometimes, of course, we may try too hard. In our search for a style we may assume a way of self-conscious acting that isn't truly our own. Here I think of a bit of dialogue in William Hanley's play *Slow Dance on the Killing Ground*. Rosie, a nineteen-year-old coed, launches into a passionate, pseudo-intellectual speech about her college thesis. As she concludes, Randall, a hip Black youth, tells her she is really "somethin' else . . . somethin' extraordinary." After a pause the exchange continues:

ROSIE.   . . . What do you mean, extraordinary? What's so extraordinary about me?
RANDALL. Oh, man, you know . . . *Style*, Rosie! You got *style*!
ROSIE.   *(Contemptuously)* Style! This isn't style! This is *front*! All front! But you hit it right on the head, Randall. A style is what you need in this life. You have to find a style and stick to it. That's my whole problem: I haven't been able to find a style yet. . . .[1]

Too often it is only a "front" we present to the world, and we, like Rosie later in the play, find that a front doesn't hold up when the going gets rough—when we are faced with death.

Rosie at least realizes the difference between style

[1] (New York: Random House, 1964), pp. 79, 80.

and front, and that is a good place to start our search. A front is only a façade that we may assume for any number of superficial reasons: gratification of certain desires, a sense of being in control, trying to be what we think others would like us to be, a need to cover up true feelings. But a front leaves us insecure and wobbly underneath because we secretly suspect what is true—nobody knows who we really are. Style, on the other hand, grows from within as well as from without, integrating the content with the form, giving the self a sense of continuity throughout its various expressions and actions.

SELF-AWARENESS

It is possible, I think, for each of us to become more aware of the self within—who we are, who we have been, who we want to be—to see through our own fronts and lay hold of forms that are appropriate and satisfying for the expression of our inner content. We can begin by looking at our own feelings and wishes. This process does not deny our relations with others but focuses on how we *feel* about ourselves and those relationships. Too often by putting up fronts, putting on masks, conforming to images, we lose touch with ourselves. When we recognize we have feelings and wishes we begin to discover a sense of identity.

After achieving this consciousness, the next major step in self-awareness is the experience that, as Rollo May puts it, "I-am-the-one-who-has-these-wishes." Not only do I have feelings, but those feelings are uniquely and indisputably *mine,* part of *my* world.

If I experience the fact that my wishes are not simply blind pushes toward someone or something, that *I* am the one who stands in this world where touch, nourishment, sexual pleasure, and relatedness may be possible between me and other persons, I can begin to see how I may do something about these wishes. This gives me the possibility of *in-sight,* or "inward sight," of seeing the world and other people in relation to myself. Thus, the previous bind of repressing wishes because I cannot stand the lack of gratification on one hand, or being compulsively pushed to their blind gratification on the other, is replaced by the fact that I myself am involved in these relationships of pleasure, love, beauty, trust. I then have the possibility of changing my own behavior to make them more possible.

[*Love and Will,* p. 266]

To change one's behavior in order to fulfill one's desires for deeper relationships is actively to shape a style for the self.

When we become truly aware of ourselves as the subjects of our own experience we open ourselves to seeing not only the past, which we carry within us, but also the future. I am not simply the sum of what I have done to date; I also am my hopes and dreams, the work I want to do, the responsibilities I want to carry out. Certainly I will have to make decisions and perform specific acts if my future goals are to be realized. But the dreaming and hoping I do will shape my decisions and my acts—will shape the style in which I express myself.

The implications of such self-awareness for our death and dying seem clear: it is my own death I must die, and I shall do the dying. Within certain limits I can shape my death by finding and living the way that best expresses my inner self. My own good death can be a goal that I achieve in my own style.

For those who have difficulty coming to this awareness, I suggest some experimentation with new ways of thinking and feeling, some exploration into different styles of expression to help discover ways to awaken the imagination. Through our imaginations we can project ourselves into the experiences of other people and see whether they are familiar to us or unfamiliar and why. We can entertain various possibilities and implications of actions and styles unlike our own and see what they reveal about us. In our dreams and fantasies we can imagine ways of dying and how they relate to ways of living.

Dying would be much easier if only people could have enough self-awareness to know what style feels comfortable and to be able to express their needs and desires to others. But if that is not possible, it becomes even more important for those of us present to the dying person, in whatever capacity, to be sensitive to the unconscious style expressed. We must give the person enough room, enough space, to shape his or her responses and actions. We must trust the dying process, knowing the dying are living toward their deaths in their own ways.

PERSONAL DIFFERENCES

The first thing we will note in our search for style is the plain fact that people are different and different people have different styles. Charles Schulz brought this reality home in a cartoon not long ago.

© 1973 United Feature Syndicate, Inc.

I also remember the caustic comment attributed to George Bernard Shaw: "Don't do unto others as you would have them do unto you. You might not have the same tastes!"

However, some styles are more open-ended than others. If we want to be free to express our talents, develop our capacities and realize our aspirations, we must find a style allowing for these possibilities. A style that stifles our creativity, incapacitates our ability to function, and interferes with our mental growth hardly leads us to the self-awareness and expression we want in life. A recent radio report noted that the people most likely to die in auto accidents are belligerent, talkative, overactive, aggressive males who drink too much, speed, and don't fasten their seat belts. In the light of these possible consequences, people with this "style" may want to find a different one!

Arnold A. Hutschnecker is one of many doctors who suggest the possible relationship between some kinds of personalities and certain types of diseases. "Clinically," he writes, "a correlation seems to exist between the disease picture and the basic personality. That is to say there is a difference in behavior in different personalities suffering and eventually dying from different somatic diseases" ("Personality Factors in Dying Patients," in *The Meaning of Death,* p. 238). In general he observes cancer patients to be emotionally passive and dependent while heart patients are often aggressive and reckless. Dr. Hutschnecker further notes that when the basic personality changes there is a change in the somatic symptoms.

While these observations are open to exceptions and modifications in each case, we do well to remember them as we journey toward self-awareness and self-expression. If a tense, hyperactive person who works under pressure is a likely candidate for an early heart attack, he or she may want to work on changing to a life-style more conducive to growth and fulfillment.

Certainly if a person is dying it is no time for us to press for major changes in life style. A change may come, depending on how much the new circumstances serve as a catalyst, but more often than not our dying is in continuity with our living. Elisabeth Kübler-Ross once described a woman who said to her, "I've been angry and rebellious my entire life! Why should you expect me to change when I'm dying?" She was not about to accept the thought of her impending death with peace.

One cannot help saying "right on!" to this woman's recognition about herself. She would have her own difficult death to die and do it in her own way. When such an awareness can be articulated it is a great help to family and hospital attendants. Rather than being so terribly distressed at not being able to help the person accept death, they can relate to her on her own terms, letting her express herself in her own style.

Some people go peacefully to sleep and die, while others fight it to the very end. Goethe is said to have died saying, "More light." But then there is Ethan Allen. The story is told that when this Revolutionary War hero lay dying, his minister said to him in soothing tones, "General Allen, the angels are waiting for you." And Ethan Allen replied, "Waiting are they? Waiting are they? Well, let 'em wait!"

LIVING AND DYING WITH STYLE

No one can avoid dying, but each of us can utilize the freedom we have to choose what for us is a good, decent, and dignified death. This means starting our preparation long before death is imminent. Dying is more a time for gathering together our present resources than for exploring new styles.

It is never too early to think about death and to be aware of alternative styles of living and dying. To help get our imaginations working, I have delineated a half-dozen life styles that seem to me basic, almost archetypal, in human experience. In the next section we will explore these different attitudes to see what implications they have for styles of dying. As I worked through their development I discovered that within each style there are different facets reflecting both positive and negative elements. By focusing on these various aspects we can imagine some of the possibilities the style might have for us.

A change in style does not necessarily mean radical alteration in our living. Each style has positive and negative elements so we can make choices within it. By entertaining various options in our imaginations we can discover which ones we want to strengthen in our own lives, ones that enable us to live more deeply and to achieve more actively the death we want.

To be sure, these six types overlap in our actual living and dying. By holding each one before us in the mirror of imagination we may be able to see those elements which we embody. With that deeper awareness we can then set about the task of integrating the fragments of our experience into the wholeness of our style—for life and death.

CREATIVE PRETENDING

As we look at the following six styles I suggest we utilize Constantin Stanislavski's creative *"if."* It is the *if,* he tells his actors, that "acts as a lever to lift us out of the world of actuality into the realm of imagination." Sometimes we are unable to imagine a different view because we think we should really believe it is true for us. The *if* lets us entertain another perspective "as if" it were true for us. Thus we have no obligation really to believe it, only to pretend it with sincerity. Because the *if* does not use fear or force, it frees us to have confidence in the honesty of a supposed situation. When we can pretend, we find ourselves aroused to natural and real responses.

Although the human emotions we experience when we imagine "what if" are not actual feelings, Stanislavski points out, they are akin to them and "seem true" because the emotions do arise from the subconscious by the prompting of our true inner feelings. He tells his actors to imagine in their own ways the "given circumstances" offered by the play about the life of the character to be enacted:

It is necessary that you really believe in the general possibilities of such a life, and then become so accustomed to it that you feel yourself close to it. If you are successful in this, you will find that 'sincere emotions,' or 'feelings that seem true' will spontaneously grow in you. [*An Actor Prepares* (New York: Theatre Arts, 1936), p. 48]

This is a very good description of what happens when we empathize with someone else: we are aroused to inner feelings akin to what the other person feels, and in that act really experience those emotions as if they were our own.

For those people who may be fearful that such activity in the world of imagination will leave them uncentered as to who they are and how they really feel, I offer a word of reassurance. In my years of acting in the theater I have discovered the "what if" to be a remarkable source of insight not only into others but into myself. When I consciously pretend, I am enabled to see ways I resemble a certain character and ways I do not. Having experienced certain emotions in the make-believe world of a play, I then can check those against my own feelings and see where they are similar and where they are not.

When we play *if,* we try on for size a different character, a different philosophy, a different point of view, a different activity, without committing ourselves to anything but honest pretending. Sometimes we come back from the venture with the awareness that we didn't resonate at all with that experience. Or we may come back with a vision of new possibilities for ourselves, a discovery of some new dimension within us.

This is what we do, of course, whenever we are really involved in an artistic experience. Reading a novel or a poem, listening to music, seeing a play or movie, we enter that world for a time; we dwell in it as if it were our own world. It is not possible really to experience everything in the world, but through the imagination we can explore far beyond the horizon of primary experience and be the richer for it.

So not only in art, but in real life we can use our *if* to find new depths and dimensions. By pretending "what if" we rehearse our questions, our fantasies, our actions, our responses, in our imaginations. And as we creatively rehearse them we may discover their true significance for us. "What if I were this person or that person, how would I feel about life and death?" "What if I could choose my own death, how would I want to die?" "What if I had a terminal illness, how would I prepare for my death?"

In the next section we will be exploring six different styles of living and their implications for styles of dying. As you read them, and afterward as you reflect on what you've read, I invite you to pretend "what if" each style were your own. Really try to lift yourself by *if* into the world of imagination where you can put yourself in those situations, dwell for a time in those worlds. At the very least, I hope you may gain some understanding of others you know who live and die in one or another of these styles. At most, I hope you may emerge from the experience with new self-awareness—with insight into a new dimension within you or some vision of a new possibility toward which you might grow as you search for your own style of living and dying.

II
IMAGINATION

Every new discovery, every new thought,
can put a new face on the world.

Carl Jung

FOR EVERYTHING THERE IS A SEASON

An Accepting Life Style that Meets Death as an Inevitable Part of Creation

For everything there is a season, and a time for every matter under heaven:
    a time to be born, and a time to die;
    a time to plant, and a time to pluck up what
        is planted;
    a time to kill, and a time to heal;
    a time to break down, and a time to build up;
    a time to weep, and a time to laugh;
    a time to mourn, and a time to dance;
    a time to cast away stones, and a time to
        gather stones together;
    a time to embrace, and a time to refrain from
        embracing;
    a time to seek, and a time to lose;
    a time to keep, and a time to cast away;
    a time to rend, and a time to sew;
    a time to keep silence, and a time to speak;
    a time to love, and a time to hate;
    a time for war, and a time for peace.
                        [Ecclesiastes 3:1-9]

The author of Ecclesiastes, and those who share this attitude, see in existence a basic, natural rhythm in which death has a rightful, forceful, inevitable place. Within this created order we are called to live a style of acceptance for whatever life brings. All things come into being and pass away. Everyone who is born will also die.

Commonplace sayings expressing this view abound on every side. "It will all come out in the wash." "It won't matter in a hundred years." "That's the way the cookie crumbles!" "The bigger they are the harder they fall!" These are all ways to articulate a sense of life as a big balance sheet where the rhythm of time makes all things come out even. "Win a few, lose a few," and everything falls into its proper place.

Within this style, however, people may express their "acceptance" of the rhythm in different ways.

For some people, acceptance takes the form of deadly resignation to the fact that nothing lasts. They put emphasis on the negative side of the balance sheet. If all good things are destined to pass away, then human life must be futile and death the end of misery. Expect nothing, and you won't be disappointed. I can still hear my grandmother saying, "Sing before you eat, cry before you sleep!" Or at some holiday gathering where we laughed and had a good time, "I just know something bad will happen because we've all been so happy!" She enjoyed herself, but was always acutely conscious that the season of joy would pass and the season of sorrow come.

Actually, this attitude dominates much of the outlook in Ecclesiastes. The first chapter of the book begins with the words, "Vanity of vanities . . . All is vanity" (1:2). Then the author goes on to verify the truth of that observation in personal experience. "I have seen everything that is done under the sun; and

68

behold, all is vanity and a striving after wind" (1:14). "For in much wisdom is much vexation, and he who increases knowledge increases sorrow" (1:18). "Then I considered all that my hands had done and the toil I had spent in doing it, and behold, all was vanity and a striving after wind, and there was nothing to be gained under the sun" (2:11).

This, of course, is "vanity" in the first meaning of the word as "any thing or act that is vain, futile, idle, or worthless." It is interesting to speculate on how the word vanity came to be used to describe being self-satisfied or proud. Could it be that vanity in the latter sense implicitly suggests the futility of such postures? The possessions I'm proud of today will be worthless tomorrow. The self I'm satisfied with today will die.

But here in Ecclesiastes vanity means outright futility. Certainly we see the raw data for this view in our own experience. Think of persons who have scrimped and saved for a house, only to be left homeless by fire or flood. Or of someone who has worked for years to save money for a special event and then is robbed of the savings. Or of someone employed many years by a company who is laid off because of declining demand or economic recession. Or of someone who has worked hard throughout life, looking forward to retirement, who dies or is killed before being able to realize that leisure. In these circumstances it is very tempting to say "nothing matters" or "there is nothing to be gained under the sun."

For the writer of Ecclesiastes the only meaning to life comes through faith in God. All of people's efforts on their own are vanity, but God gives them strength for their toil and an occasional glimpse of joy to help them through their days. Because all things come from the hand of God there is a certain consolation in the fact there is "a time for every matter under heaven." The mystery of death becomes a summons to righteous, temperate, God-fearing living. This writer's despair and sense of futility give way to a resigned acceptance in faith. In effect he seems to say: the seasons come and go, times change; the only sure thing is death, so I will accept it as a fact and be grateful for the times of happiness that may come to me.

Another, less pessimistic, variation of this "accepting" style is one that emphasizes a more practical understanding of nature and of humanity's place in it. This view is illustrated by a story a friend told me. She was visiting an elderly sister and brother who had come from a peasant family in Hungary some years ago to live in the United States. The brother, in his eighties, was feeling the weight of his years, unable to get around very well physically and with his eyesight failing. A lady from across the street was also there. The brother, weary and discouraged with his situation, finally said, "It's too hard. I wish the Lord would take me. I'm ready to go." The neighbor, in a firm, matter-of-fact voice, responded, "Well, you can't go . You can't go until it's your time. So you can't go!"

The sister in this story, Ella Patz, shared the same kind of simple and direct approach to life. She was crippled and had to walk with a crutch, but she had an independent spirit and practical nature. "We take it how it comes, Betty dear," she would say to my friend. Or, "We each have our own way." She too was "ready to go" some years before she died, but she knew she couldn't go until it was time. She lived her days in simple pleasures—a walk in the sun, bread and coffee in a big old-fashioned mug for breakfast, a little reading, a little solitaire (I'm sure she never cheated!), chuckling at television programs, darning socks, giving to us gifts of her courageous spirit in ways she never imagined. She rarely complained; she accepted where she was when she was there, and her death was part of that life.

I wonder whether the practical attitude toward life and death is one that is particularly characteristic of people who live or have lived near the land. To see crops come and go, animals being born and dying cannot help, I think, giving persons perspective on their own place in the rhythm of nature. When we personally confront the world and its seasons, there is a direct experience of growth, change, maturation, and decay. We can work within natural forces, but they operate beyond our efforts. Crop failures, floods, and other such disasters are real indeed, apart from our desires, intentions, or needs. Death, natural and accidental, is part of this given reality.

Perhaps the farther away from the land we have lived, the more emphasis we have put on man-made standards for achieving success. If persons work hard and are clever and tough enough, we surmise, they need never fail. In this framework, power and health are part of success; weakness and illness are failings. Death then becomes the greatest failure of all, to be denied as long as possible. The haunting suspicion lingers: if only we were clever enough or tough enough we could prevail against it forever.

In Enid Bagnold's play *The Chalk Garden* the grandmother, Mrs. St. Maugham, has lost touch with the task of gardening, trying to grow things in chalky soil—in her life as well as in her garden. In this passage she laments the death of some lilies to a visitor:

MRS. ST. MAUGHAM. All gone!—All—Oh—when things are killed in my garden it upsets me—as when I read every day in the newspaper that my friends die! . . .

71

MISS MADRIGAL. That is why a garden is a good lesson—
MRS. ST. MAUGHAM. What?
MISS MADRIGAL.—so much dies in it. And so often.

[Act I, End]

When we pick up our vegetables so easily in the market it is hard to remember the days of sun and rain, the human beings and machinery it took to provide them. When we buy our hamburger and (sometimes!) steak pre-wrapped in plastic it is easy to forget it came from a living steer, butchered for us. Disasters like crop failure and flood are far away; man-made problems like strikes and inflation seem more real. Perhaps through the style of Ecclesiastes we can rediscover the rhythm of the seasons and our place in the natural order.

This accepting style can be expressed in yet another way—not in negative resignation or in practical acquiescence but in what we might call "positive participation." For persons living in this perspective there is neither a passive sense of futility about life nor a patient waiting for death, but a creative embrace of the season of death when the time comes to let go of life.

In his play *A Man for All Seasons,* Robert Bolt sees this view as characteristic of Sir Thomas More. More, on his way to be executed, pauses to comfort his daughter with these words:

Have patience, Margaret, and trouble not thyself. Death comes for us all; even at our birth . . . death does but stand aside a little. And every day he looks towards us and muses somewhat to himself whether that day or the next he will draw nigh. It is the law of nature, and the will of God. [Act II, End]

Thomas More loved his family and the pleasures of

living. For years he fought for his life through the courts. But when the sentence of death was passed and he knew it was useless to struggle further, he accepted the fact that his "time to die" had come and embraced it. Indicative of More's attitude is an exchange between him and the Duke of Norfolk after he had been condemned to death by Henry VIII. "'Indignatio principis mors est. The displeasure of the prince means death,' said the Duke of Norfolk. 'If that is all, my Lord, then truly there is no other difference between Your Grace and me, other than that I will die today and you tomorrow,' was Thomas More's answer."[1]

Those who are able to participate positively in the accepting style do not arrive at that place easily or without effort. There is a book about a man dying of cancer at the age of forty-seven who wrestled the last year of his life with the paradoxes of Ecclesiastes' seasons and was finally able to say "yes" to them. In the Prologue to the book that chronicles his search, the editors, who were also his friends, make this observation:

Into the purposes of the universe, it is not so hard to fit birth, laughter, love, peace. But weeping and war, casting away, death—these are more bizarre pieces to place in their season and time. This requires work and devotion and courage. And these Mark Pelgrin gave, with a sense of genuine meaningfulness, as he moved into the time and season of his death.[2]

It is one thing to resign oneself to fate; it is quite another thing to embrace the dark side of life. Those

[1] Hans Küng, *Freiheit des Christen (The Freedom of Christians)* (Hamburg: Siebenstern Taschenbuch Verlag, 1971), p. 53.
[2] Mark Pelgrin, *And a Time to Die,* ed. Sheila Moon and Elizabeth B. Howes (Sausalito, Calif.: Contact Editions, 1962), p. xi.

who do so seem to find in their love of the light side the power that enables them to accept the other as well.

Pretend you resonate with the accepting style of Ecclesiastes; then use your imagination to explore the implications of this view. What if you really accepted all the rhythms of life, including death, as an inevitable part of creation? How would you feel about dying?

Do you feel that the repetition of the seasons leads you to doubt the meaning of any or all experiences and activities of life?

Although the seasons come and go, are they really the *same* seasons each time?

Following Ecclesiastes you can best fight pessimism by really living the basic rhythm of life which you affirm.

If it is time to embrace can you live in that time fully? If it is time to refrain from embracing can you do that also, believing there will be a time for embracing again?

Are you able to see in weeping the truth for that time, but not the truth for all time, since laughter also has its seasons and is enriched by the tears that lie on either side?

Can you imagine knowing when to let go and embrace the time of your death?

Imagine you are Woodrow Wilson saying at your death, "I am a broken piece of machinery. I am ready."

Imagine you are Leonardo da Vinci writing, "As a well-spent day brings happy sleep so life well used brings happy death."

Imagine you are the neighbor saying, "You can't go until it's your time. So you can't go."

Imagine you are Sir Thomas More comforting your daughter with the affirmation, "It is the law of nature and the will of God."

Imagine you are the author of Ecclesiastes writing, "For everything there is a season . . . a time to be born and a time to die."

"Man was made for joy and woe," William Blake said. The optimists exclude the latter; the pessimists exclude the former. The rhythm of Ecclesiastes urges a style that embraces them both.

DO NOT GO GENTLE INTO THAT GOOD NIGHT

A Defiant Life Style that Rebels Against Death as Personal Destroyer

Do not go gentle into that good night,
Old age should burn and rave at close of day;
Rage, rage against the dying of the light.

Though wise men at their end know dark is right,
Because their words had forked no lightning they
Do not go gentle into that good night.

Good men, the last wave by, crying how bright
Their frail deeds might have danced in a green bay,
Rage, rage against the dying of the light.

Wild men who caught and sang the sun in flight,
And learn, too late, they grieved it on its way,
Do not go gentle into that good night.

Grave men, near death, who see with blinding sight
Blind eyes could blaze like meteors and be gay,
Rage, rage against the dying of the light.

And you, my father, there on the sad height,
Curse, bless, me now with your fierce tears, I pray.
Do not go gentle into that good night.
Rage, rage against the dying of the light.

[Dylan Thomas, "Do not go gentle into that good night"]

If the attitude in the previous style is basically one of accepting death, the primary characteristic of this style is rebellion against death. The Dylan Thomas of this poem and those who share this view see so much to be lived for that they must reject death as the end of work, hope, possibility. To rage against the forces of darkness that conquer the human spirit, to hang on to whatever energy there is as long as possible, is to hold death off and gain time for a little more of life. After all, how is one really to know when it's time to die? There are innumerable instances in which people have struggled against immediate death and lived to tell of it. It sometimes happens that when the odds are greatest, people are challenged to struggle hardest and are victorious. Sheer, uncompromising defiance of limitations and restrictions is surely part of living.

No one can say that the person who expresses this style is not very much alive while he or she is dying. Dylan Thomas' poem can be seen as an appeal to his father for some display of passionate intensity to show that life still pulses in him. It is true that while anger and rage in a dying person are hard on family members and attendants, we often prefer them to listless passivity and silent resignation. John Hinton suggests that some patients' fight for life, no matter how hopeless, serves as their antidote to despair:

Admittedly it is hard to find much comfort in the situation of the dying man who says outright "I don't want to die" and continues a doomed struggle against incurable illness, but he may well need the hope and the refusal to surrender. Even the unavailing struggle may be preferable to the desolation of no hope at all. [*Dying* (Baltimore: Penguin Books, 1967), p. 102]

Some people can feel their own life and vitality most

in their rage and defiance—and where there is life there is hope.

Beyond its summons to his father, however, I find in Thomas' poem a fervent hymn of praise to life and its possibilities. Old men, wise men, good men, wild men, grave men—no matter how full their lives—*all* have experienced opportunities missed, understandings not perceived, marks not made on the world. To rage is to say "yes" not only to what was and the desire to hang on to it, but also to what might have been had not death interrupted. To rage is to lament the shortness of life and the fact that we don't always see what we have until we lose it.

Near the end of Samuel Beckett's *Waiting for Godot,* Didi looks at his sleeping companion, Gogo, and wonders to himself:

Was I sleeping while the others suffered? Am I sleeping now? . . . We have time to grow old. The air is full of our cries. But habit is a great deadener. At me too someone is looking, of me too someone is saying, He is sleeping, he knows nothing, let him sleep on. [Act II]

Those individuals who affirm the defiant style of life see that some rage is necessary to offset the sleeping we do in life.

Having looked at the overall context of this style as suggested in the poem, let us now explore some of the different ways the defiant style may be expressed in the lives of individuals.

On one level there are people who live only in anger. Of course, there may be strong physical reasons for the anger in persons who are dying and are at the extreme limit of their endurance. Part of the rage may be at the pain itself; part may be at the living who are preoccupied with petty aches and troubles from which they will recover.

There is a letter written by a woman with cancer which speaks candidly about the sheer difficulty of dying. Her last paragraph reads:

I've gone through it all; the early times of Hope, the Facing the Truth, the Grin-and-Bear-It Stage, then Just Bearing It, and now the End-Is-Just-Around-the-Corner or Final Stage. I'm still angry about it all, for I think no one has ever loved living more or had more fun doing it than I, and I want it to go on and on. But if it can't, then I must be truthful and say there are a few advantages in living only half a lifetime. Besides the end of good, death also means the end of tribulations—no more holding in the stomach, no more P.T.A.,no more putting up the hair in pincurls, no more Cub Scouts, no more growing old. [Carol Willis, letter in *Ladies Home Journal,* January, 1960, p. 4. © 1959 Downe Publishing, Inc.]

This woman is living her death in Thomas' style, I think, with passion and integrity. The dying have every right to feel sorry for themselves, to be angry at the disease that cuts off life before its natural time, to mourn, however ironically, the loss of even the dullest of the tribulations of living.

On another level, persons who express anger and rage at the time of death may be carrying through the style of their whole lives. Remember the story described earlier about the woman who said she had been angry and rebellious all her life and wasn't going to change because she was dying?

I remember the tenacious way my grandmother clung to life. After she was in her seventies she broke both hips and had to be cared for in a convalescent hospital, confined to a wheel chair. But she absolutely refused ever to accept her situation. Her stubborn, determined jawline was indicative of her iron will. Her prayers were often fierce demands for God to take her—but in retrospect I think she fought against that possibility with every word.

My grandmother's youngest son died in an accident when he was twenty-one and she nursed her husband through a lingering illness before he died at the age of seventy-four. But she never seemed to absorb the losses into herself. All through her life she resisted change, wanting things to be the way they once were. Her love for family was inviolate, and her commitments were held with determined loyalty. As she grew old, these qualities of strength became part of her suffering. She always talked of when she would walk again and go home. She would not adjust to the new surroundings, refusing even the distraction of watching television, an activity she had enjoyed previously at home.

I can remember visiting my grandmother and noticing the strength in her arms. Her hands worked continually—grasping the arms of her chair as she rocked back and forth, or, for some strange reason, grabbing her clothes and tearing them to shreds. Now I see that her reaching and pulling were outlets for all the energy manufactured by her defiant body. She was rending her garments as an expression of impatient rage against her infirmity. Her heart, it seemed, grew stronger. But her mind, unable to stand the tension within her, found increasing refuge in some unreal world of memory and make-believe. In the last days before her death she finally grew quiet, as though worn out at last by her passionate struggle.

I remember how hard we tried to find ways to make her comfortable and at peace, and how much my mother, especially, suffered because she could not help her. Had we realized then that my grandmother had her own death to achieve, the same hard way she lived, perhaps it would have been easier for us. Certainly this experience was one of the places I came to realize the importance of preparing ourselves now to change when necessary.

The person who has always been scrappy, with a strong sense of self-determination and a fighting spirit, will face death with the same defiance and rebellion—a style of death in continuity with the style of life. Anthony Quinn, in an interview, perceives himself this way:

"There's so much to do, so much to write about, and so little time. . . .

"'Do not go gentle into that good night,' Dylan Thomas wrote that to his father who was dying. Well, I'm not going gentle either." Tony shakes fists at heaven. "When they come for me, I'm going out kicking and raging."[1]

It is likely he will if this is his style. Perhaps, too, his self-awareness will provide new perspectives as his own death approaches.

In Rainer Maria Rilke's book *The Notebooks of Malte Laurids Brigge,* there is a description of the death of Christoph Detlev Brigge in which his dying shouts and roars can be heard all over the village:

That was not the death of just any dropsical person; it was the wicked, princely death which the chamberlain had carried within him and nourished on himself his whole life long. All excess of pride, will and lordly vigor that he himself had not been able to consume in his quiet days, had passed into his death. . . .

How the chamberlain would have looked at anyone who asked of him that he should die any other death than this. He was dying his own hard death.[2]

[1] Robert Kerwin, "Tony Quinn Prowls the City," *California Living Magazine, San Francisco Sunday Examiner and Chronicle,* April 29, 1973, p. 9.

[2] Trans. M. D. Herter Norton (New York: W. W. Norton, 1949), pp. 22, 23.

Rilke sees us carrying within ourselves throughout our lives the death that is ours to die.

On yet another level, there are those for whom this style has a different expression. They do not rebel with anger at the pain of death or at death *per se;* they actively protest the way death comes—as too soon, as unjust, as unnecessary. They do not rage against the dying of the light so much as they fear the loneliness and unknown that may come upon them when the light goes out.

The death of Jesus, as described in the New Testament, has elements of this style. In Gethsemane Jesus sweated "great drops of blood" as he prayed to have the cup of death pass from him. Though he believed in the goodness of God's will, still Jesus did not "go gentle into that good night."

Oscar Cullmann has pointed out the striking contrast between the death of Jesus and the death of Socrates. Socrates died a beautiful death, serenely talking with his friends, whereas Jesus died an agonizing death, deserted by most of his followers. "With sublime calm Socrates drinks the hemlock; but Jesus (thus says the Evangelist, Mark 15:34—we dare not gloss it over) cries: 'My God, my God, why hast thou forsaken me?' And with another inarticulate cry He dies (Mark 15:37)."[3] For the Christian the fact that Christ died sharing our human fears has given help and comfort at the time of death. It is believed that he is present with us in our anxiety and loneliness, having experienced them himself. That sense of his presence may help believers to go gentle into their good night, or, if not to go gentle, to console them in the knowledge Jesus didn't either and it was still all right.

Another illustration of this style as active protest

[3] Cullmann, *Immortality of the Soul or Resurrection of the Dead?* (London: Epworth Press, 1958), p. 24.

against the way death comes can be seen in the lives of people who are oppressed, discriminated against, or imprisoned unjustly. In these situations the loss of hope and courage can bring death quickly. Those who are able to hold on to faith in the future, to a sense of their own worth, are less likely to give up to death prematurely. In *Man's Search for Meaning: An Introduction to Logotherapy,* Viktor Frankl describes his experiences in a Nazi concentration camp. He suggests that the extreme situation brought out different styles of life for the prisoners.

Naturally only a few people were capable of reaching great spiritual heights. But a few were given the chance to attain human greatness even through their apparent worldly failure and death, an accomplishment which in ordinary circumstances they would never have achieved. . . . Most men in a concentration camp believed that the real opportunities of life had passed. Yet, in reality, there was an opportunity and a challenge. One could make a victory of those experiences, turning life into an inner triumph, or one could ignore the challenge and simply vegetate, as did a majority of the prisoners. [(New York: Washington Square Press, 1963), pp. 114, 115]

Those who gave up died, first in spirit and then in body. Those who held on defiantly survived—either to see freedom again or to achieve their death with integrity. This was not blind rage, but healthy resistance to inhuman circumstances.

What if you live in the style of defiance? Can you imagine the reasons for your anger, rage, rebellion, protest?

Do you feel angry when you think of time passing too quickly?

Do you rebel because it keeps things stirred up and you don't have to think about death? Or are you a "reluctant" rebel, believing that nothing should be taken for granted, even death?

Imagine someone saying to you, "Do not go gentle into that good night."

Imagine you are Didi in *Waiting for Godot* saying, "Habit is a great deadener. . . . Sleep on."

Imagine you are the woman dying of cancer saying, "I'm still angry about it all, for I think no one has ever loved life more than I."

Imagine you are Tony Quinn saying, "When they come for me, I'm going out kicking and raging."

If your style of life is to defy power, fate, or the gods, you will never give up too soon. Passion will run deep in you, and your will to live will be a strong guiding force. You will use up all of yourself. If anger and rage are the best expressions of your style, you will achieve your own hard death. And others who are present with you as you die may be relieved for you when death comes, bringing you peace at last.

But remember that Dylan Thomas, for all his sense of rage, still perceived death as that "good" night. You need not enter it gentle, but you need not rebel against it forever. The boundary of death is part of the reason for your passion. Imagine that it too may have its goodness—like a loving friend who lets you be angry and then welcomes you at last into a comforting embrace.

EAT, DRINK,
AND BE MERRY

A Sensual Life Style that Fears Death
as the Denial of Human Meaning

Eat, drink, and be merry,
for tomorrow we die.

[Unknown]

Rather than accepting death as inevitable or rebelling against death as the end of life, those who follow this sensual life style try to put off thinking about it. By concentrating on pleasurable experiences they seek to evade death and feelings of fear in the face of death.

"You can't take it with you!" we hear people say as they justify their getting and spending. Or "gather ye rosebuds while ye may" as they reach for gratification of their desires. Since no one knows what "tomorrow" or death holds for us, proponents of this attitude suggest living for what is immediately available. As long as we can feel the pleasurable satisfaction of sensory delights we feel alive. Only our sense of aliveness can hold the specter of death at bay.

This style has a care-free, care-less abandon about it that has great appeal) I see it arising from life viewed as a parenthesis in the middle of the unknown. This feeling is akin to the experience captured in this lyric from Maxwell Anderson and Kurt Weill's *Lost in the Stars:*

A bird of passage out of night
   Flies in at a lighted door,
Flies through and on in its darkened flight
   And then is seen no more.

This is the life of men on earth:
Out of darkness we come at birth
Into a lamplit room, and then—
Go forward into dark again.

[Act II, Scene 5]

The style is a response to the poignant sense of the transitory nature of time. By filling the lamplit room with eating, drinking, and merriment, there is a feeling of warmth within the void. Such an affirmation of life now, in the face of death's nothingness, is a courageous act.

While the emphasis on sensual experience is the dominant implication of this style, there are, as with the other styles, several different ways the attitude can be expressed in life.

The most obvious manifestation we call hedonism, a philosophy that believes in the pursuit of pleasure and the gratification of the senses.)

The real problem for the philosopher, so the advocates of hedonism insist, is not to decide what constitutes the good life. That we all know well enough: it is a life which affords us maximum enjoyment. What we need to know is how to

86

obtain the greatest pleasure in life and how to avoid the pain that seems inextricably woven into the very fabric of living.[1]

Some stress getting the pleasure and others stress avoiding the pain. In any event the motive is highly self-centered.

Some, like Freud, have observed the pleasure principle to be our most natural instinct. Indeed, which of us does not yearn for pleasurable comforts? Which of us does not respond to promises of happiness, even such frothy ones as offered by television commercials? There we are—eating a delicious meal minutes after taking a sure cure for stomach upset, enjoying a soft drink on a sandy beach with wind blowing hair in our mouths, kissing a handsome man or beautiful girl who has gargled with a delicious (or terrible) mouthwash! Every day the magic T.V. box tells us how to obtain the greatest enjoyment. Death as illness, loneliness, unlovedness can be cured—for a price.

The most intense and immediate pleasure becomes the focus of the hedonist. "Wine, women, and song," one age called it; "sex, rock, and drugs" might be today's translation. These pleasures have strong attraction because they are instantly gratifying and absorbing enough to stave off thoughts of death for a long time.

In his novel *Couples,* John Updike describes the attempts of persons in mythical suburban Tarbox to liberate themselves into hedonism. Through adultery they seek a sexual paradise as a shield against the awareness of death. "It is a happy-ending book —everybody gets what he wants," Updike has noted with irony. Yet the couples are still as frustrated and their lives as meaningless as if they hadn't.

[1] Robert F. Davidson, *Philosophies Men Live By* (New York: The Dryden Press, 1952), p. 29.

Updike's couples, like most hedonists, discover that the pursuit of physical satisfaction for its own sake eventually leaves them more and more unsatisfied. It is a well-known truism that any pleasure prolonged indefinitely becomes painful, whether eating banana cream pie, drinking milk shakes, or engaging in sex. The fallacy of hedonism is believing that the fulfillment of pleasure will bring happiness. What it brings is an insatiable desire for pleasure and an overwhelming boredom with the means by which it is satisfied. More than one budding hedonist has turned into a full-blown pessimist in later life.

Too often there is a frantic desperation in the search for gratification. This can be all-consuming for a time, but is likely to give way sooner or later either to anxiety and rage or to emptiness and ennui. Sometimes the very thought that one day the ability to enjoy pleasure will be gone prevents a person from enjoying the pleasures at hand.

There may be times when the human spirit rebels against its own attempt to fill life with pleasant distractions. One woman, dying of cancer, spoke of the ways her family tried to keep her from thinking about her illness—puzzles, cards, projects.

My contentment was in theirs and that worked fine for a while, but who wants an eternity of fun and games? The more Arnold and I could discuss our affairs and the more responsible tasks he left for me, the more creative and worthwhile I felt. Reading everything you always wanted to read was fun, until you could. I needed some direction.
[*Facing Death,* p. 46]

Many find sufficient fuel to feed the fires of their desires throughout their lives, but it was not enough for this woman as she faced her own impending death.

Hedonism is not the only expression of this style,

however. For others the sensual style of life means recognizing all experience as sense perception. Here, then, the sensual is not regarded merely as satisfaction of bodily appetites in pleasure, but rather as the whole way we apprehend the world—through sight, sound, touch, taste, smell.

Proponents of this attitude might be said to make a "turn of the sensory"—away from ego-centered self-gratification to relationship with the whole world. Our suspicion of the body and our reaction against hedonism, they say, have taken us to an overemphasis on rational thought. But if we cannot love our bodies it is unlikely we can love the world or our fellow human beings. When we try to understand the universe only by thought we are in danger of losing touch with the sacramental nature of creation and our place in it.

D. H. Lawrence expressed this feeling best, perhaps, in this line from his poem "Non-Existence": "We don't exist unless we are deeply and sensually in touch with that which can be touched but not known." "Known," that is, in a rational way. Those who live in this dimension of the sensual style feel a unity and wholeness about life and a freedom about their bodies. In their love of sensual experience they become generous "givers," rather than self-centered "takers."

Sam Keen advocates the need for a carnal or visceral theology, pointing out that as our viscera respond to external stimuli they call us to see our common humanity:

The stomach knows that what happens to one happens to all, even if the mind tries to deny it. . . .

Thus a categorical imperative issues from the viscera: "Reverence the flesh of all men as you reverence your own." . . . Men with any feeling for the inviolability of their own bodies would not tolerate the violation of other men's bodies. [*To a Dancing God* (New York: Harper, 1970), p. 153]

He sees a return to feeling, to being in touch with our own bodies, as a necessary step in the re-sensitizing of human relationships.

John Killinger suggests the play *Krapp's Last Tape* as an example of lost sensuality. Here Samuel Beckett has written of the later years of a man who tried to comprehend the world by philosophizing about it. The central character, Krapp, sits alone with a tape recorder, playing tapes of his past life in an effort to find meaning for his present. Whenever his voice on the tape starts to reveal a thought or belief he once had, however, Krapp impatiently fast-forwards the machine to a new place. With curses he mutters to himself what a stupid bastard he was. The one place that holds Krapp's attention is a passage describing an encounter he had with a girl in a small boat, their touching each other, feeling the movement of the waves, his looking into her eyes. "The girl, the thing of the flesh," Killinger observes, "that is the one oasis of meaning in the desert of his mind."

Man is so cut off from things, from the sensation of the world around him, that he has almost, inadvertently and ironically, become a thing himself, albeit a curious and highly complicated one. In his false and illusory impressions of transcendence, he has become increasingly isolated from everything, until there is no longer anything to sustain him, to feed life into him. [*The Fragile Presence: Transcendence in Modern Literature* (Philadelphia: Fortress Press, 1973), p. 99]

It is not simply fulfillment of desire, it is finding a balance with all our human faculties and senses that such sensualists see as the basis of their life style. Joy and pleasure mean fullness and completion, not just momentary gratification.

In this view death is not so much feared as accepted. If one feels whole, death too can be affirmed. In one of his poems, "Nur einen Sommer," Hölderlin expresses his desire for a single summer of such sensual fulfillment, saying he would then be willing to die.

I shall be satisfied though my lyre will not
  Accompany me down there. Once I
    Lived like the gods, and more is not needed.[2]

The recognition that "tomorrow we die" need not give rise to a frantic pursuit of eating, drinking and being merry, but can give life and the fruits of life a sweeter taste.

What Hölderlin calls "living like the gods" here and now, by our own efforts, Sam Keen calls the presence in our lives of *grace* bestowed by the "dancing God."

Incarnation, if it is anything more than a "once-upon-a-time" story, means grace is carnal, healing comes through the flesh. The primary locus of the "action of God" is in the viscera, not in ancient Israel! Otherwise, how may I understand that grace which sometimes overtakes me in looking at the sea, or in making love? [P. 144]

Our carnal nature is not anathema to Christianity; it is a necessary affirmation if we believe the "Word became flesh."

In addition to hedonistic denial and carnal acceptance, there is yet another expression of the sensual

---

[2] Quoted by Walter Kaufmann, "Existentialism and Death," *The Meaning of Death*, p. 59.

style of life. This is a view described only briefly by C. S. Lewis. Far from being a crass hedonist or a simple sensualist, Lewis was a Christian who speculated that the human soul itself gains substance through sensory experience.

What the soul cries out for is the resurrection of the senses. Even in this life matter would be nothing to us if it were not the source of sensations.

Now we already have some feeble and intermittent power of raising dead sensations from their graves. I mean, of course, memory. [Lewis, *Letters to Malcolm: Chiefly on Prayer* (New York: Harcourt, Brace and World, 1963), p. 121]

He goes on to suggest our memory may be a foretaste of the power of the soul to live on in death; perhaps the body is in the soul rather than the soul in the body as supposed by classical thought. "Matter enters our experience only by becoming sensation (when we perceive it) or conception (when we understand it). That is, by becoming soul" (p. 123). Rather than letting the pendulum swing all the way from overemphasis on rational thought to affirmation only of feeling, Lewis sees the two as necessarily interacting within us.

Here, indeed, is an imaginative rethinking of the relationship between body and soul, with implications for a sensual life style stretching beyond death. The admonition "Eat, drink, and be merry" takes on new dimensions. It says, in effect, "Drink deeply of life and all its experiences while you are alive! Enlarge your storehouse of sensations and memories before tomorrow when you die! By so doing you will be expanding your soul for its possible resurrection." The pleasures of the senses need not be merely ends in themselves, but can become the foundation for life-enrichment.

Free yourself in imagination to explore the various expressions of the sensual life style.

Do you find pleasure in physical sensation?

Do you fill your time seeking pleasurable distractions out of fear of death?

Do sensual experiences of beauty, music, smell, taste, touch give you a sense of wholeness and fulfillment?

Does being in touch with the feelings of your own body make you more sensitive to others?

Imagine different interpretations of "eating," "drinking," and "being merry."

Eating can mean stuffing ourselves with things that taste good. What about eating as appreciating the gift of food to satisfy our hunger? Or as sharing the bread of life with others?

Drinking can mean numbing our anxiety through alcohol. What about drinking as the goodness of cool water on a warm day? Or as the various ways we quench the many thirsts of our lives?

Being merry can be synonymous with never being serious. What about merriment as being courageous, cheerful, and happy in the company of friends? Or as finding joy in the simple things of life?

If you affirm the sensual life style you will say "yes" to life and to the goodness of the body. Though you may never lose your fear of death completely, you may grow to see death as a mysterious, new sensory experience for which all your sensations have prepared you.

NO ONE EVER DIED WITH WARM FEET

A Humorous Life Style that Dances with Death Around the Edges of Ultimate Mystery

As the beloved Dr. Samuel F. Upham of Drew Theological Seminary lay dying, friends and relatives were gathered about the bed. The question arose whether he was still living or not. Someone advised, "Feel his feet. No one ever died with warm feet." Dr. Upham opened an eye and said, "John Hus did." These were his last words.[1]

This story suggests several things about the humorous life style. There is the wonderful play on words, "Feel his feet. No one ever died with warm feet." Of course not. Most of us get "cold feet," figuratively as well as literally, when we approach our death! No pun intended, perhaps, but there it is for us to enjoy.

Then, for dear Dr. Samuel Upham, there is the satisfaction of the joke itself. What a marvelous gift! As he was dying, one of his friends, without realizing it, played straight man for that final punch line. We don't

[1] Simeon Stylites (Halford Luccock), "Research," *The Christian Century,* July 7, 1954, p. 817. John Hus was burned at the stake. I am grateful to Doug Adams for showing me this story.

know what happened next in the story, but I can imagine the tension was relieved and Dr. Upham's death was made a little easier.

Finally, I think, the whole story suggests a view of life that knows death as a mystery, yet trusts the mystery enough to laugh in the face of seeming defeat. Such a view looks for the resolution of the incongruities of our lives in the mystery beyond life. Christopher Fry expresses this understanding of humor and the comic spirit:

There is an angle of experience where dark is distilled into light: either here or hereafter, in or out of time: where our tragic fate finds itself with perfect pitch, and goes straight to the key which creation was composed in. And comedy senses and reaches out to this experience. It says, in effect, that, groaning as we may be, we move in the figure of a dance, and, so moving, we trace the outline of the mystery. ["Comedy," *Theatre in the Twentieth Century,* ed. Robert Corrigan (New York: Grove Press, 1963), p. 112]

There is much we don't know, including why human beings live and die. Those who profess the comic style say "yes," but it is remarkable that we can contain those unanswered questions in a sense of humor.

The attempts to analyze and explain humor and laughter are endless. We can only say the comic view is somehow intuited by the human spirit. We experience tragedy in many forms—sorrow, loss, misunderstanding, accident, frustration, fate—and it appears relentless in its course. But then, suddenly, there is a break in that inevitability of the tragic—a sense of incongruity, a juxtaposition of opposites, an element of surprise, a transcendent glimpse of human foibles and follies. In these interruptions we find humor, laughter, and delight arising from an intuition that says to us that tragedy is not the whole story. The ambiguities that would crush us in tragic perception become grist for the mills of humor.

While the comic life style arises out of mystery and incongruity, there are several ways it can be expressed.

Some people use humor in an attempt to control the mystery as much as possible. Rather than seeing wonder and delight as Christopher Fry does, they see mockery and irony. On one level they may take pleasure in elevating themselves to a position above others by insults or "put downs" (delivered lightheartedly, of course!). On another level there is the use of gallows humor or the sick joke. One example you may recall goes, "Besides that, Mrs. Lincoln, how did you like the play?" This is one way of dealing with death through humor, but the laughter is strained, macabre, a little ugly.

There is a sense of power in gallows humor—in playing it cool by cruelly mocking bitter tragedies. If we can ridicule life through derisive laughter we are not so vulnerable to it. But this expression of comedy can betray those who use it. When sick humor becomes a persistent view, it distorts the perspective on life and self that comes from compassion and understanding. Jokes inspired by contempt lose the light of laughter, and those who tell them are left only with despair.

One of the most helpful statements on the understanding of humor I have seen comes from the late writer-critic Bernard DeVoto:

Humor is one of the mind's devices for making life tolerable. No man ever made a joke about another man without divulging a joke on himself. No man ever laughed at fortune except in self-defense. . . .

Humor is a psychic adaptation: an act where action is impossible, a solvent of the insoluble, a defiance masked as surrender, a bursting-asunder of the inexorably contract-ing, a risk taken safely, pain turned to its own healing. At its simplest, it is wonderfully complex, at its most superficial, it is many strata deep and there is no such thing as idle humor. Mere puns and the all but meaningless witticisms of exhilaration are phantasies as purposeful as a child's play-ing. There is, that is to say, no such thing as a joke; there is only a pretense, perhaps only a self-deception. There is only a mind trying to establish an armistice, if but for a moment, with itself and with the world.[2]

In sick humor the joke is on the person who tells it, revealing the deep-seated fear that perhaps life is absurd and without meaning. We may laugh at the jokes for any number of equally self-revealing reasons, but the laughter has a bitter and hollow ring. (Others who affirm the comic style of life use humor as a way to handle the contradictions in their experi-ence. They find the ability to laugh at their own and other people's foibles a healthy way to keep them-selves in proper perspective. There is constructive power in such humor that can effect change in at-titudes.) Satirists, columnists, and comedians have long known this.

To see ourselves with the eyes of good humor re-quires an act of imagination, looking at ourselves from the outside—as in the poem "Jello Truck" by a friend of mine, Mark Juergensmeyer:

When I fell from the dumb cliff top
Scared by the air
Catapult and sudden rock
When I could think I thought
By God some day I'll die like that.

[2] Quoted by Elizabeth Berryhill in "Lillian Hellman's *My Mother, My Father and Me: A Critical Response," Festival Theatre Student Study Series,* Syllabus VIII (San Anselmo, Calif.: Festival Theatre, 1966), pp. 40, 41.

No daggers, heroes, relatives
And draperies, the tragic drama
Or even honest battle with a man's disease;
My luck being what it is I'll be
In a sun-drenched street
Clobbered by a Jello truck.

Having existentially felt the tragic possibility of his own death, this friend was able to turn his vision of himself and his style of death into a humorous poem. For the moment, at least, he resolved his ultimate fear into a penultimate speculation on the absurdities of life and the way they surprise us.

Reinhold Niebuhr expressed the strong relationship between transcendent humor and the mystery that surrounds us:

The intimate relation between humour and faith is derived from the fact that both deal with the incongruities of our existence. . . . Both humour and faith are expressions of the freedom of the human spirit, of its capacity to stand outside of life, and itself, and view the whole scene. . . . Laughter is our reaction to immediate incongruities and those which do not affect us essentially. Faith is the only possible response to the ultimate incongruities of existence which threaten the very meaning of our life. [*Discerning the Signs of the Times* (New York: Scribner's, 1949), p. 112]

Laughter may not resolve our questions and frustrations in an ultimate sense, but it makes them easier to bear.

I remember the marvelous ending of *The Treasure of Sierra Madre.* After the terrible ordeal of getting the gold dust from the desert hills—suffering physical deprivation, internal strife, theft, murder, insanity—the survivors make their way back to civilization. There they discover bandits have torn open the bags of gold dust, thinking them filled with sand. The treasure has merged again with the desert. They sit in despair; then they begin to laugh. It was the only possible response to make. Their laughter had a healing grace.

Finally, there are some people for whom the expression of humor as a life style encompasses even a bit of the mystery. Christopher Fry describes a dream in which a man turned the pages of the book of life, the end of which would reveal the meaning of existence. The pages were alternately tragic and comic, and as he neared the end he could scarcely wait to see which held the final answer. When he reached the last page, it turned out to be a page of comedy and the man burst into laughter as he read. He awoke from the dream, his face still holding the laugh, but as he started to tell his discovery, the meaning vanished from his memory. Fry then makes this comment: "Comedy is an escape, not from truth but from despair: a narrow escape into faith. It believes in a universal cause for delight, even though knowledge of the cause is always twitched away from under us, which leaves us to rest on our own buoyancy" ("Comedy," p. 111). This is the vision we find in Fry's own plays; the rhythm of life is tragic and comic, but the final answer lies somewhere on the side of comedy.

I think my mother knew by intuition something of this rhythm. She had more than her share of burdens and sorrows in her life, yet I remember her as loving laughter and fun. In her presence we found delight; nothing was so bad that it could not be contained in her sense of life as essentially good. I don't mean she didn't feel downhearted at times, but she never felt that way for long. After she suffered a heart attack she slowed her pace somewhat but was never inclined to live as an invalid. As far as she was able she did what she wanted to do, knowing she risked losing a few extra years.

On the morning of her last heart attack my sister and I stood at her hospital bed, unaware of what was happening. There was no last gasp as the movies portray; there was movement as we held her hands, then a gradual slipping away. As I've lived that moment over and over I have tried to feel what my mother may have experienced in those moments. Did she know we were there? Was she afraid? I know there was pain and physical distress, difficulty in her breathing. But did she know?

I think now that what we saw on my mother's face was surprise. "Well, we certainly didn't expect this! On this day? In this place? In this way?" It was not and is not funny. I do not laugh; I weep with the memory. But I believe my mother's delight with life and her wonder at the unexpected turns it could take was the style in which she danced with the mystery. That she was surprised out of life does not seem inappropriate.

People affirming the humorous life style in this broad understanding find in that experience a metaphor for existence and a source of transcending insight. Arthur Koestler points to this possibility in beginning his study of *The Act of Creation* with an analysis of laughter.

Laughter is a reflex, but unique in that it serves no apparent biological purpose; one might call it a luxury reflex. Its only utilitarian function, as far as one can see, is to provide temporary relief from utilitarian pressures. On the evolutionary level where laughter arises, an element of frivolity seems to creep into a humourless universe governed by the laws of thermodynamics and the survival of the fittest. [*The Act of Creation: A Study of the Conscious and Unconscious in Science and Art* (New York: Dell, 1964), p. 31]

Because laughter arises from surprise, from seeing ambiguity, from sensing we have been fooled, it heralds the "flash of insight" at the heart of every creative act. Habitual response is defeated by originality and spontaneity. Man is no static creature, slave to mere instinct and biological urge. He is capable of laughter and therefore of discovery and insight.

What Koestler describes scientifically, Fry has imagined artistically. In *The Lady's Not for Burning* Thomas Mendip says to Jennet Jourdemayne, "For God's sake, shall we laugh?" She says, "For what reason?" and he replies:

For the reason of laughter, since laughter is surely
The surest touch of genius in creation.
Would *you* ever have thought of it, I ask you,
If you had been making man, stuffing him full
Of such hopping greeds and passions that he has
To blow himself to pieces as often as he
Conveniently can manage it—would it also
Have occurred to you to make him burst himself
With such a phenomenon as cachinnation?
That same laughter, madam, is an irrelevancy
Which almost amounts to revelation.[3]

Imagine yourself within the humorous life style. How do you feel about the contradictions and incongruities of living?

What kinds of jokes do you tell, and what do they say about you?

Do you laugh most easily and freely in surprise and delight or in ridicule and mockery?

Do you find in humor a source of insight, discovery, and revelation?

[3] Christopher Fry, *The Lady's Not for Burning* (London: Oxford University Press, 1949), p. 49. Reprinted by permission of the publisher.

Imagine yourself as a comedian. Which one would you choose to be and why?

Imagine yourself as one of the people at the end of *The Treasure of Sierra Madre.* Could you laugh as the gold dust blows away?

Imagine that the answer to the mystery of living and dying is contained in comedy. What do you see?

Of all the creatures, human beings seem to have the greatest, perhaps the only, capacity for humor. It is this gift that puts us a little lower than the angels, and through which we can say "yes" to life and death with all their ambiguities and surprises and contradictions. In "The Hound of Heaven," Francis Thompson speaks of hiding from God "under running laughter." Perhaps that laughter is the music for our dancing.

GOOD NIGHT, SWEET PRINCE

A Tragic Life Style that Experiences Death as Always Too Soon

Hamlet. O! I die, Horatio;
   The potent poison quite o'er-crows my spirit:
   I cannot live to hear the news from England,
   But I do prophesy the election lights
   On Fortinbras: He has my dying voice;
   So tell him, with the occurrents, more and less,
   Which have solicited—The rest is silence.

Horatio. Now cracks a noble heart. Good-
   night, sweet prince,
   And flights of angels sing thee to thy rest!
                                    [Act V, Scene II]

"Something is rotten in the state of Denmark." "The time is out of joint." Prince Hamlet arrives home from the University to avenge his father's death by ridding Denmark of the man who killed him: Claudius, the King's own brother, who now sits upon the throne, married to Hamlet's mother. But avenge how and when? As Hamlet wrestles with these questions he is

103

plunged into deep despair, filled with questions about the meaning of life. Prompted by visions of his father's ghost, his will hardens and he settles on a course of action. In the events that follow—some willed, some accidental—Hamlet has his revenge, but many others die as well, including in the end his mother and himself.

What is Hamlet's tragedy? That he cares so much—his father murdered, his mother deceived, the throne usurped? That he wants revenge? That he is indecisive and sensitively moody, unable to kill Claudius when he has the chance as his uncle kneels at prayer? That there are so many unintended consequences—Polonius killed by mistake, Ophelia's madness and death, Laertes' desire for revenge, Hamlet's mother drinking the poison intended for him?

Certainly all these are tragic elements. But our deep sense of tragedy at the end of the play is, in Wordsworth's phrase, "felt in the blood, and felt along the heart." It is the feeling that Hamlet is dead too soon; that he and others are victims of events that should never have happened. Claudius let his ambition lead him to murder. Hamlet's reaction became an action filled with confusion and ambiguity, with good intentions gone awry, with disastrous consequences and accidental twists of fate. His father's ghost is laid to rest and the people are saved, but Hamlet himself is slain, never to see the new life Fortinbras will bring to Denmark.

If the humorous life style meets death with a buoyant lightheartedness, the tragic life style in contrast, mourns in death the sadness and brevity of finite experience. In the former there is affirmation of the wonder in life and of our ability to laugh at the incongruities. In the latter there is awareness that no matter how nobly we struggle against our limitations we will suffer and die, often too soon, victims of circumstances largely beyond our control. Tragic knowledge recognizes that things are never quite equal. No matter how hard we try, there are still efforts that do not succeed.

But there is a paradox as well. In the tragic vision we not only perceive that life is full of thwarted aspirations, unfulfilled dreams, and untimely death. We also have the sense that life has a grandeur and humanity a greatness, that both events and persons are nobler than we often experience them. If persons only got what they deserved, then it wouldn't matter and we wouldn't care. Even the extreme nihilists who avow all is nothing may be expressing their belief that they missed something—that something was there and they were cheated of its fulfillment.

Strangely enough, people realize their grandeur and nobility as they actually suffer their suffering. "Tragedy's one essential," Edith Hamilton suggests in *The Great Age of Greek Literature,* "is a soul that can feel greatly. Given such a one any catastrophe may be tragic." It is partly because Hamlet was so conscious of his actions and responses, because he cared deeply and passionately, that we grieve his loss. So, too, wherever there is suffering for what might have been and isn't, regardless of the reason, we have the heart of the tragic vision.

There are those who would describe tragedy only in the classical terms of ancient Greece. But I am not alone, I think, in locating tragic perception in the *feeling* experience of humanity. George Steiner sees this possibility. In the conclusion of his book *The Death of Tragedy* (New York: Hill & Wang, 1961), he describes a performance of Helene Weigel and the East Berlin ensemble in *Mutter Courage.* At the end soldiers bring in a dead body they think is her son and try to force her to identify it. Mother Courage stares blankly at the body of her son and silently shakes her head in denial. After the soldiers start off with the body, Steiner writes that

Weigel looked the other way and tore her mouth wide open. The shape of the gesture was that of the screaming horse in Picasso's *Guernica.* The sound that came out was raw and terrible beyond any description I could give of it. But, in fact, there was no sound. Nothing. The sound was total silence. It was silence which screamed and screamed through the whole theatre so that the audience lowered its head as before a gust of wind. And that scream inside the silence seemed to me to be the same as Cassandra's when she divines the reek of blood in the house of Atreus. It was the same wild cry with which the tragic imagination first marked our sense of life. The same wild and pure lament over man's inhumanity and waste of man. The curve of tragedy is, perhaps, unbroken. [P. 354]

We cannot all be a Hamlet or a Mother Courage, but we all experience the myriad tragedies that beset human life.

From this perspective let us look at ways people express the tragic life style in their attitudes.

For some people, the tragic view is seen primarily in terms of sorrow and poignancy. It is associated with unhappy endings, with suffering and lonely death, with time passing too quickly. In the movie *Limelight* the character played by Charlie Chaplin speaks of "a feeling of sad dignity." And in another place he says "We are all part of the human crusade—written in water."

This expression of the tragic style sees time as too short to accomplish all we want to do. This is not pessimistic pathos where we are only victims of overpowering forces. Here, rather, is the awareness of positive action and struggle that death interrupts. Jeannde Herst, a choreographer friend of mine, described a dance on death she plans to stage. Her description of what she sees runs as follows:

A man is onstage painting what gradually becomes discernible as a big orange circle. In the background we hear a clock ticking. The man rushes here and there, mixing paint, painting a little, examining his work. Then just when the circle is almost complete an alarm rings on the clock. The man looks up in surprised dismay and says, "Oh, no!" He crumples on the floor and is silent. The painting blows off the stand. ["Scenario for a Dance." Unpublished.]

This artistic vision poignantly captures the experience of the unfinished business of our lives. We work on our many projects but die before they are completed. And the more active we are, the more we leave undone.

For other people, the tragic style rests in our condition as creatures conscious of our own death. That which makes us human also gives us pain and suffering. Miguel de Unamuno, in the *Tragic Sense of Life*, puts his reflections in this perspective. The life force in each of us gives us a hunger for immortality while reason tells us life as we know it ends in death. "For living is one thing and knowing is another; . . . perhaps there is such an opposition between the two that we may say that everything vital is anti-rational, not merely irrational, and that everything rational is anti-vital. And this is the basis of the tragic sense of life" (p. 34). We cannot escape our own contradictory natures.

In the comic style we explored Christopher Fry's affirmation that the answer to existence is in the comic spirit. Here we may see through the eyes of S. N. Behrman that the answer may lie in the tragic spirit. Not long before his death Behrman said in an interview he believed every good comedy had to have a tragic background. He called attention to the terrible pain that underlies the last scene of the Jean Giraudoux play he adapted, *Amphitryon 38*. In this scene Jupiter offers to reveal the future to the very human Alkmena, assuring her it will be a happy one. She replies: "No! No! . . . I know what a happy future consists of. My beloved husband will live and die. My dear son will be born and live and die. I shall live and die."[1] In an earlier speech in the play Jupiter talks about being a god and not a man, saying, "But we miss something, Mercury—undoubtedly we miss something—the poignance of the transient—the intimation of mortality—that sweet sadness of grasping at something you cannot hold—" (p. 98). Within our humanity lies the ability to feel deeply; finitude makes us human, but also includes our death.

For others, the tragic style involves the recognition that we must go down into the depth of the human condition before we can rise again with fuller awareness. Francis Fergusson in *The Idea of a Theatre* describes the tragic rhythm of life as purpose, passion (or suffering), and perception. We begin an action with purpose, we suffer the thwarting of that purpose and emerge with new insight.

This tragic rhythm is true for all of us, not just for the royal people of classical Greek and Elizabethan tragedy. Whereas the tragic heroes of those plays suffered for the benefit of their cities, today we know that all of us suffer for one another. Arthur Miller is one playwright who has given form to the tragic style for

[1] (New York: Random House, 1938), p. 171.

our time. Responding to the charge that Willie Loman in *Death of a Salesman* lacked tragic stature, Miller said: "I had not understood that these matters are measured by Greco-Elizabethan paragraphs which hold no mention of insurance payments, front porches, refrigerator fan belts, steering knuckles, Chevrolets, and visions seen not through the portals of Delphi but in the blue flame of the hot-water heater."[2] Like Willie Loman, we all are subjects for modern tragedy: we live with unrealized dreams, we suffer the consequences of misplaced values, we gain new insights, we die too soon.

I experience again my father dying of cancer in a mental hospital at the age of sixty-two, my nephew killed in a motorcycle accident at the age of nineteen, and the silent scream of Mother Courage rises within me. And I know that others feel the scream too.

But being conscious of the tragic rhythm of life means seeing human potentiality as well as the limits of human finitude. Though our purposes are thwarted we do find new perceptions by wrestling with the obstacles. Though the odds are insurmountable, we may achieve a victory through defeat, for to act in the face of defeat is to affirm our freedom and to oppose meaningless suffering. Though we have limitations we still can struggle and pass to others the fruits of our struggles. Though we feel deeply the "slings and arrows of outrageous fortune," we still can choose to bear our ills with dignity.

Hamlet cannot live to hear the news from England, but by his action and his death he has changed the old course of history and made possible the new. "If it is man's fate to go down inevitably into suffering and death, some exultation nevertheless rises to the skies.

[2]"Introduction," *Arthur Miller's Collected Plays* (New York: Viking Press, 1960), p. 31.

Man may be crushed, but the human spirit is forever indestructible." [3]

In his final suffering my father discovered a sense of dignity and courage that I will never forget. In my nephew's short life he embraced a vitality and an experience of the wild joy at the heart of life that lives on in us who knew him.

And who of us, knowing we die, would choose never to have been born? Or, knowing those we love die, would choose never to have had their presence at all? Very few, for to have lived is something and not nothing. We mourn the deaths of all who die, old as well as young, since all fall short of realizing their dreams, or could have dreamed yet new dreams, or missed their opportunity to dream. Yet they had life, which is something and not nothing.

Jack London has left for those who affirm the tragic style some thoughts that might well be a creed calling for a new sense of the grandeur of life and humanity. He spoke these words to some reporters a few days before he died. They first appeared in the *San Francisco Bulletin* on December 2, 1916, some ten days after his death.

I would rather be ashes than dust!
I would rather that my spark should burn out in a brilliant blaze than it should be stifled by dryrot.
I would rather be a superb meteor, every atom of me in magnificent glow, than a sleepy and permanent planet. The proper function of man is to live, not to exist. I shall not waste my days in trying to prolong them. I shall use my time.

Imagine yours is the tragic style. How do you experience tragedy in life?

[3] Stanley Hyman, "The Tragic Vision," *The Saturday Evening Post,* June 13, 1959, p. 54.

Do you believe suffering is without meaning? Or that it must be without meaning?

Can you gain new insights and perceptions from your experiences of thwarted aspirations and unrealized dreams?

Can you envision death as the finite boundary that gives life its grandeur and nobility?

Imagine you are the man painting the orange circle, and the alarm rings before you have finished.

Imagine you are Hamlet saying, "I shall not live to hear the news from England."

Imagine you are Jack London saying, "I would rather be ashes than dust! . . . I shall not waste my days in trying to prolong them."

If there are any persons who can achieve their own death with style they are the tragic figures. Such persons act to affirm their personal dignity and beliefs at the risk of possible destruction. Hamlet, Martin Luther King, the Kennedys, Willie Loman—all died too soon, but their spirits are "forever indestructible."

COME NOW, GREATEST OF FEASTS

A Questing Life Style that Seeks to Find in Death the Meaning of Existence

Come now, thou greatest of feasts on the journey to free-
     dom eternal;
death, cast aside all the burdensome chains, and demolish
the walls of our temporal body, the walls of our souls that
     are blinded,
so that at last we may see that which here remains hidden.
Freedom, how long we have sought thee in discipline,
     action, and suffering;
dying, we now may behold thee revealed in the Lord.
[Dietrich Bonhoeffer, "Stations on the Road to Freedom,"
Letters and Papers from Prison]

Dietrich Bonhoeffer, a German pastor-theologian, wrote this poem in a Nazi concentration camp where he had been imprisoned for his part in a plot to assassinate Adolf Hitler. When the plot failed he was one of many members of the resistance movement in Germany to be implicated and arrested. Bonhoeffer underwent eighteen months of interrogation and was sentenced to death by personal order of Heinrich Himmler. He was executed at Flossenburg on April 9,

1945, a week before American forces liberated the camp.

Bonhoeffer was a "quester." In this poem he describes his whole life as a quest for freedom. He reflects on the various shapes his search took —discipline, action, suffering, and, finally, death. He did not drop one form as he turned to another, but rather absorbed each "station" into the next in a continuous journey. The fulfillment of the quest in death was for him an affirmation of his belief in God as the Lord of death as well as life.

Focusing neither on the humorous nor the tragic, this style reflects the search for the meaning of existence in the entire rhythm of life. It contains both comedy and tragedy as consummated in the reality of death itself.

Inherent in the questing style is a persistent exploration of all life's possibilities. Here is no quiet acceptance of the seasons and whatever may come. A restless yearning to satisfy some inner need plagues us to look into the heart of existence. "Itchy feet" some call it and take to the road in their search. "Inquiring minds" others describe it and pursue a variety of philosophies. "Restless hearts" still others say as they seek to find that cause above all others to which they may devote themselves.

Underlying the search is the nagging suspicion that the answer may rest in death itself, or beyond. That there is a boundary we can cross only by dying gives strength to that suspicion. There is no absolute assurance we will find anything on the other side. Still the boundary awaits our arrival, reminding us that all quests go by that way and whatever meaning we have found will be fulfilled in that end.

It takes some of us a long time to discover that death may hold the meaning of existence for which we seek. I had an experience of this possibility a few years ago through an act of imagination. The occasion was a guided fantasy trip through my life—past, present, future. A group of us was asked to close our eyes and then to fantasize through memory or imagination our feelings at different ages in our lives. The whole event is still very vivid to me. I was lying on my back in the grass under some trees, and my fantasies ran as follows:

Newborn baby:	big—warm—light—soft—fed—good—helpless
Age 5:	big—alien—lonely
Age 12:	old for age—reflect a lot on life—make something of myself—need attention—make a place
Age 25:	good—create together—integrity—community—shared responsibility
Age 45:	too late—haven't discovered what it all means
Age 65:	older than my mother when she died—knowing is knowing you don't know
Old:	"I'll tell you a mystery"[1]
Very old and dying:	thought it would get dark, but sensation of brightness—brighter and brighter—maybe now I'll know what it means!

This sense that the meaning of life will be made clear in death did not leave me feeling that the search here and now is any less important. It did give me assurance that perhaps we are not frustrated forever, that someday our search will be fulfilled.

[1] This is the last line of a play by Clifford Odets, *The Flowering Peach,* spoken by Noah after reflecting on what he learned on the Ark and receiving the rainbow as God's promise not to destroy the world again.

(Those who live in the questing style may express different attitudes and discover different meanings.

Some will emphasize the search itself. Here is an openness to challenge, to change, to new, unknown experiences.)Tennyson's poem "Ulysses" summons us to risk a life of continuing discovery:

> . . . Come, my friends,
> 'Tis not too late to seek a newer world.
> Push off, and sitting well in order smite
> The sounding furrows; for my purpose holds
> To sail beyond the sunset, and the baths
> Of all the western stars, until I die.

For the adventurers the quest is enough. The search continues into death and is intense *because* we die.

Lord Balfour visualized death itself "as an adventure—a great, new oncoming experience." Can we be sure we know nothing in death? It may be we *can* experience the very moment of dying itself and enter some new realm of perception. This is not to say people with this attitude want to die. But they do not fear death so much as they anticipate some new possibility that only dying will reveal. On the tomb of T. S. Eliot in Westminster Abbey is this inscription, taken from his *Four Quartets:*

> . . . the communication
> Of the dead is tongued with fire beyond
>   the language of the living.

And Henry James, we are told, met his death with the words: "So here it is at last, the Distinguished Thing."

This embrace of new experience may have a negative manifestation for those who find it a summons to seek their own death actively. If a person is inclined to despondency, death may seem to provide a "solu-

115

tion" to the problems of living. Or if a person is seeking "highs" of expanded awareness through drugs, he or she may turn to death as a new experience. The negative expression of the quest for fulfillment in death may mean a conscious reaching for death in suicide or an unconscious flirting with dangerous acts that may lead to accidents.

For others the questing life style takes the form of a search for personal wholeness. Arthur Miller suggests that the question underlying every great drama might well be "How may a man make of the outside world a home?" How may I live so that I have a sense of oneness with life—a feeling of completion in myself and a feeling of belonging with others in creation? How may I live so that each day is good enough to have been the last?

The quest for "home" is a familiar one. And the moments when we arrive there are peak experiences. George Leonard, in *The Transformation* (New York: Delacorte Press, 1972), talks of the possibility of transformation whenever we achieve this heightened awareness: "And after all the journeying, all the pain and joy, we may discover that the Transformation was difficult to grasp, not because it was so far away but because it was so very near. To find the immense world of delight is, in the end, to come home again, where it always was" (p. 237). Such a feeling of being whole in oneself, in the world, presupposes, I think, the belief that life was created by a beneficent force that wishes us well and not by a hostile force that wishes us ill. Though we may oftentimes feel like aliens in a strange land, our quest for home is not a futile one.

Those who carry on their quest as Christians find their wholeness and their home through faith in Jesus Christ. H. Richard Niebuhr writes in *The Responsible*

Self that when the Christian "feels and knows himself to be a son of God, an heir in the universe, at home in the world, he knows this sonship, this at-homeness, as not only like Jesus Christ's but as actualized by him " (p. 176). Believers find their home within God's own person, now and always. The quest finds meaning through the life of faith; its fulfillment in death is the entrance into eternal life in God's love.

Ruth Hoffman, dying of cancer in a California hospital, can say, "I am ready. We all have to die. I'm a good Christian and I've learned that the closer one lives to God, the happier one becomes as the end draws near." And Hermann Lange can write to his parents on the eve of his execution by the Nazis: "I am, first, in a joyous mood, and, second, filled with great anticipation. . . . There will be no more secrets nor tormenting puzzles. Today is the great day on which I return to the home of my Father . . ."[2]

Finally, there are still others who emphasize in their quest a commitment to the cause of human need in community and history. It is a quest the individual undertakes out of concerned belief and love for others. Here is the person of action who climbs the mountain not simply as the adventurer, because it is there, but because it must be climbed in pursuit of certain goals. Better still, if the mountain is in the way of some good it is regarded as a thing to be moved.

Such a search involves personal risk and suffering. It leaves one open to criticism and ridicule, as well as to heavier penalties when the quest is directed toward change in society and its laws. Yet for committed persons there is no choice; they must endure the hardships and welcome them as necessary. Thus

[2]Quoted in *Dying We Live*, ed. Hellmut Gollwitzer, Käthe Kuhn, and Reinhold Schneider; trans. Reinhard C. Kuhn (New York: The Seabury Press, 1968), p. 93.

117

Daniel and Philip Berrigan voice their opposition to war in "A Sermon from Prison":

We choose peace, not in rhetoric alone, but in truth, love, in risk, suffering, in every element of our lives. Even if that meant loss of possession, public disgrace, prison, death. To lose that others might gain, to be imprisoned that others might be free, to die that others might live, this is the stuff of life, this is humanity in its fullest glory. [*America Is Hard to Find* (Garden City, N. Y.: Doubleday, 1972), p. 106]

The struggle goes on wherever human life and dignity are involved: for peace; for racial justice; for equal opportunity; for freedom from oppression, sickness, and ignorance. And it goes on in many ways—in the organizational efforts of people like Eleanor Roosevelt and Dag Hammarskjöld, in the legal confrontations of Martin Luther King and Ralph Nader, in the radical protests of the Berrigan brothers and Cesar Chavez.

Those who undertake this questing life style in pursuit of social change live often on the edge of uncertainty and in the shadow of death. Martin Luther King knew his life was in danger; yet his commitment was stronger than his fear. In accepting the 1964 Nobel Peace Prize, Dr. King could say:

I have the audacity to believe that peoples everywhere can have three meals a day for their bodies, education and culture for their minds, and dignity, equality and freedom for their spirits. I believe that what self-centered men have torn down men other-centered can build up. I still believe that one day mankind will bow before the altars of God and be crowned triumphant over war and bloodshed, and non-violent redemptive goodwill will proclaim the rule of the land. . . . I still believe that we shall overcome.

For such persons death becomes the seal of their lives and the measure of their belief. Many of them must have made the decision to die in their cause and thus be freed from fear of death in order to pursue the course of action necessary.

Martin Luther King and Dietrich Bonhoeffer are rightly called martyrs. That is, their lives were consummated in the faithful witness of their deaths. Martyrdom is not a style in itself, but can be the result of the questing life committed to a cause. To set out to become a martyr is more a "suicide mission" than a quest for meaning. Real martyrs do not seek death for its own sake, but choose to accept death as a possible consequence.

Imagine for yourself the questing life style. What form do you see it take?

Do you seek new challenges and embrace new discoveries? Can you imagine your death as a new experience?

Is the search itself enough, or do you anticipate finding the meaning of life in your death?

What are the causes of your life to which you are committed? Is there any cause for which you would choose to die?

Do you believe in a form of eternal life? Does that belief or lack of belief affect the way you live and search?

Take a fantasy trip backward and forward in your life to see if you can capture some of your feelings as to where your search has taken you and will take you in the future.

Imagine you are Hermann Lange on the eve of your execution saying, "Today is the great day on which I return to the home of my Father."

Imagine you are Martin Luther King saying, "I still believe that we shall overcome."

Imagine you are Dietrich Bonhoeffer saying of death, "Come now, thou greatest of feasts on the journey to freedom eternal."

Those of us who reach the place in our quest where we can die without overwhelming fear know also that no one can have power over us. Since the threat of death is often the worst thing we can imagine, that threat may tempt us to betray our commitments. But if the quest has brought peace with the fact of death we may be able to anticipate the fulfillment of our search for meaning in the free acceptance of death when the time comes. William Stringfellow came back from the threshold of his own death with this new perception:

Life is a gift which death does not vitiate or void: faith is the acceptance, honoring, rejoicing in that gift. That being so, in my own story, *it did not matter whether I died.* Read no resignation or indifference into this confession. It is freedom from moral bondage to death that enables a man to live humanly and to die at any moment without concern.
[*A Second Birthday* (Garden City, N.Y.: Doubleday, 1970), p. 203]

III
ACHIEVEMENT

As life and love are an art,
the ability to die is also an art.

Jürgen Moltmann

ACHIEVING OUR DEATH

When in later life the attention is withdrawn from the external world it may be that the life-energy gathers itself together for its last and most significant creative act. The human being *himself* becomes the recipient of his own life-energy. He is liberated from identification with the outer world. He is free, as Whitman sings, "with the delicious near-by freedom of death" and like a free man can devote himself to the final task of his life which is—to use Jung's phrase—the *achievement* of Death. [M. Esther Harding, *The Way of All Women* (New York: G. P. Putman's Sons, 1970), p. 263]

Until his death at eighty-five, Carl Jung pressed for a sense of continuing growth in self-awareness. Only in this way would we give proper meaning to the evening of life as well as to the morning and the afternoon. In the above quote Esther Harding carries on Jung's vision—emphasizing the way the human organism rallies to new heights even as life crumbles.

"... Last and most creative act ... recipient of own life-energy ... the final task of life ... the *achievement* of death." The words leap at me from the page as a challenge and a summons. Rather than focusing on what I can't do—stop death, not be anxious—I will focus on what I *can* do—admit death into my life *now,* prepare myself for that last creative act *now*. The word "end" means not only a conclusion; it means also a goal. I will try to make my end my own and achieve that goal in my own style.

There are those who will say it doesn't matter when or how we die because all of us are bound to die our own death. I would agree that each of us dies a personal death, but not that it doesn't matter. There is that within me which seeks to use my freedom to its limit, which seeks for a sense of completion *to* my life as well as *in* my life. I affirm with Robert Browning:

I would hate that death bandaged my eyes, and forebore,
And bade me creep past.
No! let me taste the whole of it . . .

I do not expect to be able to control completely my dying. Rather, I would hope to imagine the goal, contemplate its achievement, and let the end fill the now so that I can fit the present and the future together in continuity of style.

At a conference on death and grief, Dr. Edwin Shneidman described an "appropriate death" as "one which permits a person to die in a way that is better than the way he would have died if he hadn't seen where he was in the flow of things." This suggests what Carl Jung means by achieving death. It is part of what I mean when I speak of dying with style.

THROUGH THE MIND'S EYE

The major key to discovering one's style is the freedom and flexibility of the imagination. Hamlet says he thinks he sees his dead father and in answer to the question "Where?" replies, "In my mind's eye, Horatio." This is the mysterious power by which we can see and hear and feel beyond the limits of our immediate time and place.

In the last section we explored six life styles by trying them on in our imagination. (By imagining the way another person lives and dies I expand my experience and come to greater awareness of myself and my possibilities. By imagining the way I want to express myself I gain greater freedom to choose what I do and how I do it.)

(I can imagine the thing I fear most about dying and death, and as I live with that experience it may become less fearful. I can even imagine alternatives to what I fear most and live with those experiences also.)

(Those six styles of life and death set forth in the previous section do not exhaust the possibilities. Each of us will discover an outward form for inner content that is individual and unique. Most of us will probably come to the conclusion that our style is a mixture.)I recognize there is a bit of each style reflected in me: I think the first is basically true; I urge the second for others who are dying; I suspect the third has the right idea; I take refuge in the fourth; I imagine myself in the fifth; and I aspire to the sixth!

(If we can consciously grasp the form with which we are most comfortable and choose ways to develop the strengths of that style we will be on the way to achieving our best death. Something of this intention can be seen in the German prayer: *"O Herr, gib jedem seinen eigen Tod"* ("O God, give to each his own death").

(The form we discover should not be rigid by any means. We all change with circumstance, age, understanding, experience.)Death as an event at the age of thirty is different from death at age thirty-one, not to mention age seventy-five. Once we have discovered a general shape and style that is the best expression at a given time, we can use it as a good point of departure for subsequent modifications.

Seeing our selves through the mind's eye of imagination can enable several things to happen necessary to our achievement of death.

First, we gain a deeper sense of our own identity and continuity. I am the subject of my imaginings, and I remain constant. I see in *my mind's* eye, and my mind belongs to me. I don't become other lives I imagine; I participate in their styles by pretending "what if" I lived that way—and it is *I* who pretends. Rather than losing identity in this process, we experience the identity more directly and with more continuity. This self dies; this continuity becomes the achievement at the end.

Second, through imagination we will know better our true feelings, and be better able to respond to them. When I imagine my own death or any death in a certain style, I have a feeling response that I can choose to accept or reject. It may be an emotional reaction to which I say, "Why do I feel so strongly there?" and proceed to new insight. It may be a faint perception of a way I'd like to be and subsequent pursuit of possible changes to make it more accessible. I may even choose to don a mask so that others don't see the real me, or pretend I have feelings I don't really have. But at least I will be choosing consciously to do so.

Third, in the mind's eye we can get a sense of ourselves as agents who are active in our own living. Not only am I the subject who imagines and the subject who feels, I am also the subject who acts. What I choose to do makes a difference in what happens to me. When I interact with others I experience different qualities of living. I can choose to give up my life for a cause or for someone else. In the light of my own inevitable death I can act now in life to achieve that end. "A determinate future is not a feal future," John Macmurray reminds us in *The Self as Agent.* "The real future is the indeterminate which is determined in action. . . ." My choices shape my future.

Seeing my self through the mind's eye of imagination enables me to become aware of my style and judge whether it is an appropriate style for expressing my whole self as an imaginative, feeling doer in the world. This kind of integration is not simply growth in terms of old categories. We need to be transformed so that we can look at death as the end to be achieved.

And how is that to happen? As George Leonard perceives, "Awareness *is* the Transformation," because the deeper sense of self it brings changes the way we see our world. If we fear death, then, how else can we transform that fear except by becoming aware of our feelings as we share the rhythm of living and dying at the heart of creation? And how better to become aware than by exercising the imagination?

"It is the imagination," Christopher Fry suggests,

which makes the world seem new to us every day, which peoples history with living men and women, and transforms geographical charts into fresh winds, treacherous currents, and the ancient tracks of traders who felt and suffered as we do. It is the imagination which awakens the dry bones of any subject to sing about the mystery of creation. ["On Keeping the Sense of Wonder," *Vogue Magazine,* January, 1956, p. 158]

But where do you see the mystery of creation that empowers you toward achieving your own death in dignity and style? "In my mind's eye, Horatio!"

IN MY OWN WAY

When we can imagine achieving our own death, we will be on the way to finding the appropriate style. Where the sense of personal identity is strongest, the style will be most clearly defined. Erik Erikson calls this "integrity."

Although aware of the relativity of all the various life styles which have given meaning to human striving, the possessor of integrity is ready to defend the dignity of his own life style against all physical and economic threats. For he knows that an individual life is the accidental coincidence of but one life cycle with but one segment of history, and that for him all human integrity stands and falls with the one style of integrity of which he partakes. [*Identity: Youth and Crisis* (New York: W. W. Norton, 1968), pp. 139, 140]

Achieving our own death requires individual integrity; that is, it requires us to assume responsibility for our own life.

Terminal illness may be a strong rallying point for raising the self to greater awareness of its integrity. Compressed time can have a depth that lets us realize our selves in ways it might take years to discover. This is why children or young people who are dying often show a maturity and wisdom beyond their years.

We meet the crisis of death with the same identity and resources with which we meet other crises. But where there is a strong desire to achieve one's death with dignity, the old elements can become reintegrated in a new way. Lillian Smith wrote of the new insights she gained from her long struggle with cancer.

But life opened for me, too. . . . The experience of facing my awesome anxiety, then the things you go through again and again (not too painful, remember; painful, yes, but not unendurably so); then death, learning not to fear it really, any more; learning that pain can actually be forgotten especially when one is writing or concerned about others;

128

learning that there is a strange energy inside one that pulls pulls pulls.[1]

For those whose lives run the full span of their years, who die when the tissues wear out and the organs are used up, there is a different concern. While they have longer to discover their essential identity and style, they also must hold on to it longer and suffer the erosion of the body that houses consciousness, awareness, integrity. We all know people who, as they deteriorate physically, cease to be the people we knew before. In the mystery of personhood we cannot say where their other "selves" have gone or at what point they achieve death. When the complexities of life are too much to bear, yet the body doesn't die, perhaps it is an achievement to let the mind go until the body is ready to follow.

Most of us derive satisfaction from completing various tasks in life. Those who work with dying patients observe in them a need to tie up the loose ends of their living, to finish their unfinished business. Part of achieving my death in my own way will involve how I relate to the need for "closure." Much anxiety about death comes from fear of what will happen to our bodies and to our families. Rather than preventing the dying from talking about these matters they should have opportunity to participate in making decisions—adjustments in the home, financial arrangements, the funeral or memorial service.

I do not mean pressing a dying person for decisions too difficult because of pain or emotional stress. There are some people who will not choose as their way such conscious decision-making in final matters. Directly, or indirectly by doing nothing to raise the

[1] Quoted by George P. Brockway, "You Do It Because You Love Somebody," *Saturday Review,* October 22, 1966, p. 53.

issues, they will leave these matters in the hands of others. These wishes should be respected also.

"Truly this is my grief and I must bear it," Jeremiah says in the Old Testament. Each of us must face death and grief as an individual. All through our lives there are things others can do for us, but life requires that each of us die. Someone can give his or her life for me in certain situations, thus delaying my time of death. But ultimately no one can die in my place as me.

But while the last act of dying is the task of the self alone, it may be we need never see ourselves as completely alone. Where we have known loving relationships, where others have been present to us and we to them, then we are surrounded by their continuing love and presence into our dying. I act alone in my death, but in my memory I recover the reality of those loving experiences, and in my imagination I can feel them now. Alone but not alone, for the love I have known goes with me, sustaining me in my "last and most significant creative act."

WITH HELP FROM OTHERS

Although all of us must achieve our own death, this does not mean others can't help. We are always persons in community with other persons. We become who we are through the many relationships of our lives, with family and friends as well as in the interaction and interdependence of society. So in our dying we need continuing fellowship and support.

Each of us has to find the appropriate ways to help others in dying, as in living; the needs will vary according to the individuals and the circumstances. Most important, we need to stay present to one another. Many people have noted that when someone was known to have a terminal illness, friends gradually dropped away after a flurry of concern —embarrassed or frightened or at a loss for words. At a time when community is important this isolation only impedes the achievement of death.

It is crucial to give one another the opportunity to talk—about anything we desire. This is the time to express our wishes, to work through relationships and feelings, to understand angers and to recall the love of family and friends. It is neither heartless nor inappropriate to talk about dying to a dying person if that is what is wanted. After all, it is the primary focus of the person's life for this time.

Persons who have been reticent or inarticulate about their feelings will need special consideration. They will not become talkative overnight. But if we allow an openness in sharing, they will express themselves in their own way.

Sometimes our sheer presence means more than words. Physical touch is one of the most comforting ways to share—holding hands, touching the cheek, hugging—all these warm expressions communicate care and concern. Physical touch also conveys our acceptance of the dying person. We do not shrink from the death that is at work; we share it in our embrace. If the pain is too great and physical touching a burden, we shall need to find other ways to touch—by reading aloud or playing records, by looking at pictures or resting a hand on the bed or chair.

It is important to talk, especially to the elderly, about their past—what they did and where they lived; to look at photographs and share experiences from earlier days. This need is expressed vividly—of all places!—in a mystery story by Agatha Christie:

Miss Blacklock sat up at last. Her face was swollen and blotched with tears.

131

"I'm sorry," she said. "It—it just came over me. What I've lost. She—she was the only link with the past, you see. The only one who—who remembered. Now that she's gone I'm quite alone."

"I know what you mean," said Miss Marple. "One is alone when the last one who remembers is gone. I have nephews and nieces and kind friends—but there's no one who knew me as a young girl—no one who belongs to the old days. I've been alone for quite a long time now." [*A Murder Is Announced* (New York: Pocket Books, 1951), pp. 131, 132]

This is a poignant but real experience. As we grow older, our identity includes awareness of ourselves as young, middle-aged, *and* old. For others to recognize this is important to our sense of continuity.

Some may feel it too painful to look at the past and relive old memories. But if we could be willing to share such experiences we would find a joy in rediscovering the past that is greater than the pain. A difficult and seemingly empty present can be revived and filled with people and events we had forgotten.

We can help one another talk about the deeper meanings and beliefs of our lives, about our imaginings concerning death. Above all, as Thornton Wilder says, we should extol the world to one another. Here Julius Caesar sits with a dying friend:

Another hour has gone by. We talked. I am no stranger to deathbeds. To those in pain one talks about themselves; to those of clear mind one praises the world that they are quitting. There is no dignity in leaving a despicable world and the dying are often fearful lest life was not worth the efforts it had cost them. I am never short of subjects to praise. [*The Ides of March,* p. 145]

Let us not be conspirators in silence, fearing to upset others by talking about life and death. Let us help one another in the ways we need.

I remember George, a male nurse in the hospital where a friend of mine spent the last weeks of his struggle with cancer. George was helpful in countless ways: assisting him to shower, lifting him to remake the bed, sharing gossip (George's wife was a cook in the hospital kitchen!), chatting about events of the day. My friend grew weaker and finally could neither eat nor speak. On the morning he died George brought him some apple juice and asked if he would like to thank God for it. My friend nodded yes, so George said a prayer and helped him drink the juice. Then he went to sleep and died a short time later. When I talked to George in the afternoon he told me he felt privileged to be present with people who are dying: "I like to just put my arms around them, and love them into the kingdom!"

To achieve our death in our own most appropriate way, we need physical help to ensure minimal pain. The more vulnerable we are to suffering the more dependent we are on others to help make us comfortable and do what we cannot do for ourselves. We also need emotional help. The familiarity of home is ideal, but in any case the dying should be surrounded with helpful pictures, music, or desirable "things."

Finally, we can give one another hope—for possible remission of the disease, for days without pain, for a good death. However, we must also let go when the time of death is near. One man expressed his agony in a weak voice: "I want to sleep, sleep, sleep and not wake up. How can a man die in peace when everyone wants him to get well?"[2] We must take our cue from the dying. Sometimes before the end the person begins to withdraw, to become detached. When that happens we must not let our grief and love become a

[2]David Hendin, *Death as a Fact of Life* (New York: W. W. Norton, 1973), p. 98.

burden. Each of us works a personal achievement in a unique style—with help from others.

MAKING A COVENANT

The task then is to achieve our death as persons living in community. We must seek to relate both to our own attitude toward death and to our relationships with others. I have found it helpful to think of these two focal points as covenants to which I am committed.

A covenant is an agreement entered into on a basis of mutual understanding and trust, a promise made to be faithful and loving to others or an Other in response to faithfulness and love received. A covenantal relationship implies more than contracts or bargains because it suggests a growing interaction tempered with grace, blessing, and peace. I am obedient and steadfast to the terms of a covenant not because they are legally binding but because I choose to be responsible to the meanings and values I have affirmed. Furthermore, a covenant gives me direction; it evokes response and enables me to see my future goal as part of my present.

By consciously considering the act of covenanting we may be led to reconsider elements of our style that interfere with achieving our death. For instance, persons who are "loners" covenant unconsciously with others in ways to insure their privacy and isolation. But perhaps they do not want to die under those conditions. Then I think they would make conscious efforts to get their relationships on a different footing. They will reshape their covenants toward the style they want to achieve.

One of the covenants we make in our dying is with other people—family, friends and those who may attend us in illness. In the task of achieving our death in the most appropriate way we covenant with them in recognition of mutual needs. In this relationship I recognize how hard my dying is for them. While their grief and sympathy and presence are supportive to me, I give back understanding and comfort as best I can. In covenant I recognize and appreciate the gifts of friends and the skills of physicians. I ask them to help me have less pain, to be comfortable, to sustain my life while that is worthwhile. But I promise to remember that they cannot resolve my ultimate difficulties. The deeper issues of joy, peace, and fulfillment depend on our relationship.

In covenant we seek to hold on to one another as long as possible and then to let go when it becomes appropriate. Robert Kavanaugh describes this need: "First, the dying person needs to receive permission to pass away from every important person he will leave behind. Only then can the patient begin to deal with his second problem, the need to voluntarily let go of every person and possession he holds dear" (*Facing Death,* p. 75). This need for permission to die may seem strange at first. But the tears, the helplessness, the need of the living can cause the dying to feel guilty for "copping out." Certainly the granting of permission to die is not a thing to be given easily. Persons dying do not want others to give them up too soon. But neither do they want others to make them feel they can stop dying and get well if they try harder. There may be initial shock as self-pity and mutual resentments emerge: "You're dying and leaving me!" "But you'll be living and I won't!" But then there can be honest sharing of the situation as it is, mutual mourning and common memories to sustain the mourning. Gradually, in covenant, they are enabled to take leave of each other.

The other covenant we must enter if we are to

achieve our death is a covenant with death itself, or perhaps with oneself in dying if that wording is more helpful. The terms of this agreement will be in keeping with our covenant with life. Every life style includes an attitude for encountering death in keeping with that style. If we affirm death as part of life and therefore good if life is good, then a covenant with death becomes a vital part of that affirmation.

Our covenant with death means accepting death into life where we are, absorbing the final end into the joy and pain of being here and now. As Paul Tillich has written: "If death is accepted by us already, we need not wait for it, be it near or far, with fear or with contempt. We know what it is because we have accepted it in all its darkness and tragedy. We know it is the confirmation that we are creatures and that our end belongs to us."[3] We will not risk accidents or end our lives prematurely, but neither will we squirrel ourselves away for the winter, afraid to live at all. We know our life moves toward its end, yet we use our time and achieve our end by accepting it now. We are freed from undue anxiety and excessive self-protection.

In covenanting with our death we rid ourselves of the pseudo-deaths of the spirit that rob our lives of vitality. We promise to live life fully, now. Who knows what new possibility may yet come? I once heard Dr. Kübler-Ross tell of an eighty-three-year-old man who asked her to pray for the Lord to take him soon. When she returned about four weeks later he urgently asked her if she had prayed. She said, "No," and he replied with relief, "Good!" It seems he had fallen in love with a seventy-eight-year-old woman across the hall and didn't want to die after all.

[3] "That They May Have Life," *Christianity and Crisis*, September 21, 1964, p. 174.

But even where there is no hope for new possibilities, there is the present with its own immediate pleasures and joys: a little less pain from time to time, cold apple juice, the sun, visitors. However little time a person has left, it is too much to waste in despair or anxiety. One woman said in a film interview, "The radiation treatments made my eyelashes, eyebrows, and hair all fall out. But those are little things. . . . I have good days and bad days—who doesn't?"

In a covenant with death, suffering takes on new meaning. "In the course of my illness," William Stringfellow writes, "pain threatened to become both occupation and preoccupation. By the time that I was no longer able to work in any ordinary sense and was seeking small diversions in the Sears catalog or by baking bread, I began to realize that, in truth, *pain had become my work" (A Second Birthday*, p. 55). Thus we do not berate ourselves for lack of productivity. By giving attention to the "work" of pain we do what is possible to relieve it with medicine or distraction and commend ourselves on work well done.

Our covenant with death also involves our religious beliefs. H. Richard Niebuhr defines "revelation in our history" as "that special occasion which provides us with an image by means of which all the occasions of personal and common life become intelligible."[4] Perhaps, then, we covenant with that image through which we understand all our living—as well as our dying. For Albert Camus this revelatory image was personal freedom in the face of absurdity. For me the image is the person of Jesus Christ, in whose life, death, and resurrection I see the activity of God as a loving creator. This life, freely given to me, is good, and nothing happens to me outside a loving concern. Therefore the death that waits is part of God's will. To

[4] *The Meaning of Revelation* (New York: Macmillan, 1941), p. 109.

achieve my death in dignity is my "fitting response" to this intention for my life. In my covenant with death, to use H. Richard Niebuhr's phrase. I am reconciled to the "Determiner of my Destiny."

COME, SWEET DEATH

"Komm, süsser Tod," resound the words of the Bach chorale. "Come, sweet Death." How can there ever be such a petition, when life is so precious, so infinitely fascinating, so wondrous, and so filled with people we love?

For some, the call for death to come sweetly may be a final act of defiance: "I have done my best and I know death will win, so come on! Come sweet (O 'bittersweet!') death and have done with it."

For others, it is a prayer for an end to pain and agony. Those who wrestle with fatal disease often go through a process of withdrawing from the world —saying goodbye to family and friends and to the things of their lives. When those tasks are completed, the unfinished business taken care of, and all has been said that needs to be said, then death comes as a blessing.

The moment of death is not often a crisis of distress for the dying person. For most, the suffering is over a while before they die. Already some of the living functions have failed and full consciousness usually goes early. Before the last moments of life there comes a quieter phase of surrender, the body appears to abdicate peacefully, no longer attempting to survive. Life then slips away so that few are aware of the final advent of their own death.

[John Hinton, *Dying,* p. 77]

It is rare that a person is happy to die, but when there is no longer a need to prolong life and continue suffering, then sweet death may come as a welcome stranger. John Keats achieved his death from tuberculosis at the early age of twenty-eight, yet he was ready. As he lay dying in Rome, Keats comforted his friend who sat with him, saying, "Severn, lift me up, I am dying. I shall die easy. Don't be frightened. Thank God it has come."

For others whose bodies are worn out and whose hearts are tired, death may come as the friend who sets them free. W. H. Auden wrote of such a vision:

Let even the old rejoice
The Bleak and the Dim, abandoned
By impulse and regret,
Are startled out of their lives;
For to footsteps long expected
(There's a Way. There's a Voice.)
Their ruins echo, yet
The Demolisher arrives
Singing and dancing.
["For the Time Being"]

"Come, sweet death" may be a prayer for the release by which my achievement of death is actualized. We may be "startled out of our lives" by singing and dancing!

The task of achieving our death varies from person to person and from one circumstance to another. Most of us will probably, at some point, in some way, say, "Come, sweet death." Not too soon, not until we've drunk the last drop of goodness we can manage. But at last, for most of us, the covenant will mean making peace with the end, and may even mean hoping for goodness beyond our death.

It does not necessarily take a long time to get ready to die. We can talk about what is real and important in a few minutes. Or we may have the opportunity to

139

prepare ourselves over a whole lifetime. Dying itself is a kind of summing-up time, when we become the "recipients of our own life-energy" and turn inward to do our work and make our peace. But the style by which we reach the final achievement will be an extension of the one we have evolved in life—as Leonardo da Vinci perceived when he said, "I thought I was learning how to live and all the time I was learning how to die."

DYING AND LIVING
IN DEATH

It was then it struck Oleg that Shulubin was not delirious, that he'd recognized him and was reminding him of their last conversation before the operation. He had said, "Sometimes I feel quite distinctly that what is inside me is not all of me. There's something else, sublime, quite inde-structible, some tiny fragment of the universal spirit. Don't you feel that?"[1]

"Not all of me shall die," Pushkin wrote in one of his poems, voicing a feeling that haunts most of us, in-cluding Shulubin in Solzhenitsyn's novel. Which of us has not been grasped by a strong refusal to believe that all consciousness ends with death? It simply is not possible that I—all of me—will cease to be one day! This "thing," this "essence," this "me," which I experience growing and feeling through changes yet with continuity—how can this "me" be lost forever?

Yet the reality of death cuts across our lives again and again. We see the dead body, devoid of life, and we do not know where the "person" has gone. It is

---

[1] Alexander Solzhenitsyn, *Cancer Ward,* trans. Nicholas Bethell and David Burg (New York: Bantam Books, 1972), p. 483.

indeed "the undiscover'd country, from whose bourn no traveller returns."

In spite of this fact of death the conviction persists that there is something "indestructible," some "tiny fragment of the universal spirit" that continues when our bodies die. Edward Hoagland emerged from a period when death was very real to him with this insight: "I realized more distinctly than at any time in years that . . . I believed in some form of reincarnation or immortality—this a conviction, not a wish."[2] Here is no formal religious belief in an afterlife, but a strong, almost primitive sense of personal, ongoing life force.

It is hard to believe the accumulated experiences and memories of a life can abruptly end. It is equally hard to believe there is no new realm of growth for those who die young or some second chance for those with unfulfilled lives. Kurt Vonnegut, Jr. was asked about a character named Kilgore Trout in one of his novels. He replied:

He is modeled after a character in Mark Twain—a man who wrote secretly and hid his life's work in a trunk. The trunk and its contents were destroyed after the man died. Nobody ever read a word he wrote, and yet he was allowed to lead the parade of writers, Shakespeare and all the rest in Paradise. ["Ask Them Yourself," *Family Weekly*, October 28, 1973]

This projection, albeit a whimsical one, satisfies some longing in our hearts. It seems right and just to think we may find after death a proper recognition for the secret places of our lives.

It is hard to dismiss the thought of something after death as only wishful thinking. Why should we have such thoughts at all? Observable facts tell us that persons are no more when their bodies die. Yet we

[2] "'No Groveling, Death!'," *Newsweek,* July 30, 1973, p. 9.

may have a strong, almost irrational sense of their presence after death. One "scientifically disposed colleague" wrote to William Ernest Hocking when his wife died:

Since her death I have had a very simple faith that somehow her existence is not closed. There is a "more" and she inhabits it: this seems to me too certain to be shaken by pure reason. I find reason groping blindly after experience, these days . . . I have felt too deeply to be discouraged any longer by mere logic. [Hocking, *The Meaning of Immortality in Human Experience* (New York: Harper, 1957), p. 190]

This conviction appears to be more than mere refusal to accept reality. Having a sense of life beyond dying seems inherent in our natures. Indeed, our intuitive assurance of some form of survival after death may be an intimation of a greater reality beyond reason.

Before considering some ways we live in death, let us look more closely at what we call *living* and *life.*

DEFINING LIVING AND LIFE

Not only is it difficult to define what *death* is, we also have problems when it comes to defining *life.* There is no way to get outside life to look at it from another perspective. Our vision is limited because we can only view it from within.

We can explain life and death, therefore, only in relation to each other, as *Webster's New World Dictionary* illustrates when it says *life* is "the quality that distinguishes a living animal or plant from inorganic matter or a dead organism." Or, *living* is "alive, having life; not dead."

In experience we can discern generally when a person is dead and when he is alive, but what is it precisely that makes the difference? Where does life come from, and where does it go? The Old Testament offers one possibility: "Then the Lord God formed man of dust from the ground, and breathed into his nostrils the breath of life; and man became a living being" (Genesis 2:7).

Clearly we are more than our bodies. What about our histories and our memories? What about our life in relation to others? To be sure, we receive sensations through our bodies. There are also such functions as thought, feeling, and will. And beyond, there is a wholeness uniting these elements that is the living person or the "spirit."

But there is an important distinction to be made in the quality of living. A person may have life in the sense of merely "existing" rather than living in any abundant, fulfilling way. Or we may say a person is living day by day—eating, sleeping, drinking—but has no real "life" in the sense of vitality, energy, animation.

In Part I we looked at ways persons are dying or dead while still alive. Is it possible that people also are alive or living in death? T. S. Eliot catches this experience for us in these lines from "Four Quartets":

We die with the dying:
See, they depart, and we go with them.
We are born with the dead:
See, they return, and bring us with them.

The dead do not cease to be for us, but carry us with them—into darkness and despair, into hope and light. We die with them (though we still live and breathe), and in time we feel reborn in life with the spirit of those dead living in our bones and blood.

It may even be that awareness continues into death. No one knows what happens in a person's innermost being as dying occurs. Is there no activity in the brain, even in a coma? If brain waves cease altogether, do we have ways to measure the "spirit" of the person and determine how and when it departs? Joseph W. Mathews relates this experience as he viewed his father's body in the casket:

It happened when I reached down to straighten my father's tie. There was my father. Not the remains, not the body of my father, but my father. ... It was my father there experiencing his death. It was my Papa involved in the Mystery in his death as he had been involved in the Mystery in his life. I say there he was related to the same Final Mystery in death as in life. Somehow the dichotomy between living and dying was overcome. ["The Time My Father Died," *motive,* January-February, 1964]

I am not saying death is not real, or that bodies shouldn't be pronounced dead and be buried. I am saying we cannot be sure there is no continuity for the spirit when the body dies.

It is possible to accept death as final and at the same time to believe there is something more we cannot see because we still have bodies. All the ways we die and live in death are open to our imaginations. Let us then imagine them without restriction. As we do so we may locate a focal point for our intuitive sense that something about us lives into and beyond our death. We may also discover new possibilities for our living here and now.

THROUGH THE MINDS OF PEOPLE

One of the ways a person continues living after dying is in the minds and hearts of others. We live in the memories of individuals—family members, friends, acquaintances. We live also in the effect of our deeds and actions in the history of mankind.

Many times those who die continue to have great

power over the living. This continuing influence may be stifling, like domineering parents who continue in death to force their children to act in ways the parents want. Or survivors may be left with great feelings of guilt in relation to persons who die—feelings that affect on an unconscious level the way the living conduct their lives.

The person who dies may be experienced by others as an ongoing presence. One of the characters in Solzhenitsyn's *Cancer Ward* felt this way about her long-dead fiancé: "It was not that she felt eternally bound by her promise, 'I shall always be yours.' It was more that someone you have once been very close to never entirely dies. He is still present, seeing a little, hearing a little; in fact he exists. Helpless and word-less, he will see you betray him." This continuing presence of the dead in life had a negative affect on one still living. The sense of presence can be positive as well, as it is for Christians who feel that the spirit of Jesus continues to live in their midst, enabling them to discover a more abundant life. Whether the feeling of ongoing presence inhibits or enhances the life of the living seems to depend on the attitudes of the people in the relationship. A young man condemned to death by the Nazis was able to write to his sweetheart:

Promise me that the thought of me will never stand between you and life. Remember that I am in you a reason for being; and if I leave you, that means merely that this reason lives on by itself. It should be a healthy and natural thing, it should not take up too much room, and after a while, when larger and more important things take its place, it should fade into the background and become nothing more than a small element in a soil full of potential for development and happiness. [Kim Malthe-Bruun, quoted in *Dying We Live*, p. 82]

There are also many ways a community or nation continues to experience the effect of a person's life: writings, actions, and the consequences of those actions. The work of artists lives after them in books, paintings, poems, plays, sculpture—and may have great influence years after the author has died. The deeds of people live on, consciously for a while, then absorbed into the unconscious style of the race. Those who have been active in developing strong social programs leave their influence behind. I think especially of people like Eleanor Roosevelt, at whose memorial service Adlai Stevenson said: "It is not an irreverence, I trust, to say that the immortality Mrs. Roosevelt would have valued most would be found in the deeds and visions her life inspired in others. . . ."

Perhaps when greatness has been manifest in an individual's life it is never completely lost from history or creation. Stephen Spender suggests this perspective in the last stanza of his poem "I think continually of those who were truly great."

Near the snow, near the sun, in the highest fields
See how these names are fêted by the waving grass
And by the streamers of white cloud
And whispers of wind in the listening sky.
The names of those who in their lives fought for life,
Who wore at their hearts the fire's centre.
Born of the sun they travelled a short while towards the sun,
And left the vivid air signed with their honour.

The influence of others lives on in honor and in the power of their commitment, as well as in specific deeds of goodness.

John Donne used the image that we are all part of the body, the continent of mankind: "Do not send to know for whom the bell tolls, it tolls for thee." A friend of mine expressed a similar sentiment. Not long ago his sister died, and he walked around the cemetery where she was to be buried, looking at the graves of people he had known. "Yes," he said, "I saw many old friends there." And a twenty-two-year-old man who was dying of leukemia whispered to his mother: "Do something for me? Leave a little early. Walk a few blocks and look at the sky. Walk in the world for me. . . ." We all walk in the world for one another. Everyone we know who dies becomes part of us.

ON THE EARTH

Another way we continue living in death revolves around experiences of life on earth—immortality in natural elements, in life energy, or in the individual soul.

The first of these we see among those who believe the ongoing natural world is the primary reality. Here emphasis is on simple return to the dust from which we all come. The fulfillment of this belief has been frustrated by modern-day "seal tight" metal caskets and concrete grave liners! One's body chemicals could get back to the earth when people were buried in plain wooden boxes. More and more, I hear people expressing a desire to be cremated and have their ashes scattered—in the sea, on a hillside. This is the present-day attempt to recapture a sense of the natural merging of the body's elements with those of the earth. For many people there is satisfaction in the thought that their bodies will become a source for new life in the world of nature.

Others envision not only a return of the physical elements to oneness with nature, but a return of life energy as well. This feeling is captured in one of e. e. cummings' poems:

when god lets my body be

From each brave eye shall sprout a tree
fruit that dangles therefrom

the purpled world will dance upon
Between my lips which did sing

a rose shall beget the spring
that maidens whom passion wastes

will lay between their little breasts
My strong fingers beneath the snow

Into strenuous birds shall go
my love walking in the grass

their wings will touch with her face
and all the while shall my heart be

With the bulge and nuzzle of the sea

Here all the power of a person's spirit continues to have a part in the ongoing surge of the life force.

This sense of a life force freed by death is seen by some to be a huge energy field of love. Even when we, in whom the memory of others has been absorbed, die, the love itself continues. At the end of Thornton Wilder's *Bridge of San Luis Rey* the Abbess thinks about the five people who died on the bridge and of the few who remember them.

"Even now," she thought, "almost no one remembers Esteban and Pepita, but myself. Camila alone remembers her Uncle Pio and her son; this woman, her mother. But soon we shall die and all memory of those five will have left the earth, and we ourselves shall be loved for a while and forgotten. But the love will have been enough; all those impulses of love return to the love that made them. Even memory is not necessary for love. There is a land of the living and a land of the dead and the bridge is love, the only survival, the only meaning."

Perhaps the love we have given and received is the energy that lives on when our dust returns to the earth and our atoms merge with the rest of creation.

Another view of continuing life on earth sees the individual soul as eternal, moving to another body when the present one dies. This process of reincarnation or transmigration of souls may be regarded as a simple transfer, or it may be seen in a highly complex framework of religious doctrine.

The belief in reincarnation has been present in some form throughout our history: among primitive peoples who often thought human spirits and animal spirits passed back and forth, in some forms of Greek religious thought, and especially in the major Eastern religions. Both Hinduism and Buddhism stress the undesirable nature of reincarnation, since it keeps us in a life of pain and suffering.

In the modern Western world, however, reincarnation is desirable. In each person is an immortal soul that will be reborn into another body. Supporting this belief are common experiences of *déjà vu,* that uneasy feeling of having been in a place before or having done a particular thing before. Or unexplained phenomena: people under hypnosis talking in languages they don't know; people in trances providing information about past times and places; clairvoyant experiences of people's previous lives.

But many see reincarnation simply as a way they will continue living in death on this earth. As one person said, "It is unthinkable that this one life is the only chance we get. We must have other lives to live."

IN THE ATTENTION OF GOD

Yet another view of life after death is found in what Christians call "eternal life." This is not the inevitable survival of a person's immortal soul (although some people use eternal life and immortality as inter-changeable terms); it is a belief that God gives us new life beyond death. Thus death is a real end to life as we know it. Every person dies completely. But the Lord of life is the Lord of death as well; by God's power and love we are made new creations.

Central to Christian faith are the life, death, and resurrection of Jesus Christ. In him we know God in our midst as loving and caring.

It is here my own imagination comes to life, and my own spirit starts to resonate. Living in memory and living in nature are not enough to fulfill my hunger for life beyond death, and I cannot sense within me some "immortal soul" existing apart from the whole me. I *am* able to imagine that the God who created this life can create another one. Though this belief does not de-stroy all my fears, it enables me to trust the power that makes possible my living and dying—even my fear-ing.

When asked "What is death?" Hugh Vernon White said, "Death is a movement within the attention of God, and his attention is his love." I can think of no better way to describe the affirmation about death as I understand it in terms of Christian faith. Here is no attempt to gloss over the reality of death as a final, awesome event. But death itself is the transition by which we go from life to eternal life.

It is not "heaven" but the kingdom of heaven that is the destination. Heaven is a mythological place; the kingdom of God is the non-mythological but spiritual home of the human spirit; it is the life of God himself. "Worlds" are the creations of God; he creates such worlds as fit his purpose. But God himself is the ground of our existence; life eternal is life in God.[3]

[3] Hugh Vernon White, *Truth and the Person in Christian Theology* (New York: Oxford University Press, 1963), p. 214.

Created for eternal life in God, Christians are called to a faith, hope, and love that enable them to see the eternal dimension to their selves even now.

Thus we need not try to imagine another life that has the same patterns as this one. We already know that the spirit of a person is more than the natural body. While we do not know the form of our new creation, we can anticipate some of the qualities that may be manifest in eternity, based on our experience of God's love and care for us now.

For one thing, we believe our life in God will be personal. What I am and have become im my time will continue living. Eternity is sometimes thought of as the simultaneous co-inherence of past, present, and future. God is the Lord of time, and in God's attention my time is fulfilled in all its dimensions. We have fleeting glimpses of this experience now in those moments when we feel whole and centered; when, like a lightning flash, we sense the meaning of all things and know it is good.

For another thing, we believe the life we are given in eternity will be loving. God in Jesus Christ has been revealed as the one who heals us and reconciles us to one another and to ourselves. God shares our suffering, our grief, our pain, our death in Jesus Christ. Because God's love has been made incarnate in human life we are assured of the divine presence with us in all times, in death as well as life.

Also, we believe eternal life will be a life of fellowship in covenant with God the creator. Those who have died before us are already part of the "cloud of witnesses" who share in the new creation. We have experienced the God of Jesus Christ as an active God who creates, redeems, reconciles. We will not merge into some eternal changelessness, but rather, as William Ernest Hocking suggests, participate "in partnership with him that continually labors and creates, world without end. . . ."

The belief in eternal life rests finally on an affirmation of God's action in creation as we know it now. It is, after all, *all* a mystery—life as well as death! No one can explain where life comes from any more than we can explain why death is part of life. Beyond our living in death through the memories of other people and in the recycling processes of nature, there may well be a new realm we cannot see until we have achieved our death. Then perhaps we will know the fullness of eternal life with the God of all creation.

MEMORIAL CELEBRATIONS

The way we look at dying and living in death will affect how we feel about the funeral or memorial service—or whatever we call the event that marks the death and burial of the body. There are people who feel funerals are an unnecessary, if not barbaric, custom. However, I believe they are important to our sense of the achievement of death both for ourselves and for the other people in our lives.

For one thing, the funeral or memorial service allows us to share together, in an overt way, the death of someone we knew and loved. It is our chance to acknowledge openly and in fellowship a special relationship. Here the community as well as the family needs the opportunity to recognize the passing of a person from its midst. A few years ago a friend of ours died while on vacation in Hawaii. His body was cremated and the ashes scattered there. No service was held at home. Those of us who had known and worked with him found it difficult to believe he was dead. We missed having a time to gather together and affirm what his life meant to us and to mourn his loss from our community.

153

The wider group of friends and acquaintances can also give comfort and sustaining friendship to the immediate family during its experience of acute grief. When life has been disrupted by death, the gathering of friends provides a context of continuity. Living goes on without one of its members, but it does go on, and the friends who gather make that visible.

For the immediate family, the funeral or memorial service can become a focal point for pulling together its common history with the dead. As memories and experiences are shared together among those who best knew and loved the person who has died the pain and grief are made bearable. When Mark, my nineteen-year-old nephew, was killed in a motorcycle accident we clung to one another in stunned disbelief, trying to find some place to stand as the ground rocked under us. Talking, doing what needed to be done, comforting one another were all outlets for the terrible emotional turmoil. Then as we planned the funeral we were summoned to steady ourselves and one another, to remember what was important to our common life. Mark's two older brothers spent the night before the service pouring their feelings into an affirmation of their brother's life. It was shared with those who gathered at the funeral the next day—a true gift of love in which we all participated.

I have known people who were aware they were dying and planned in advance the funeral service they wanted for themselves. Where this is possible and the person is able, I think such personal involvement is a great idea. If we are to achieve our death in the style that is ours, why not the service also? Where this has happened there is usually little of the mournful solemnity that often pervades the usual funeral. Most of us want to be remembered with joy. Certainly people can be sad and cry if they want to at my service (it appeals to my dramatic sense!), but I want them also to laugh and celebrate the fact I lived. My only regret in thinking about it is that I won't be there—I've always hated to miss out on anything!

At the very least we should give guidance as to our wishes: suggestions for hymns, poems, location, people who might participate, open or closed casket. And when we participate in planning a service for someone else we should try to capture some of his or her style and be sure to include suggestions given by the person who has died.

We will always have to be sensitive to the needs of the individual situation. Plans for a large service would be inappropriate for families new in a community who don't know many people or for the very elderly who have outlived most or all their family and friends. An intimate gathering of a few people may be an opportunity for personal sharing aloud among the group. It is important to remember that the funeral need never be rigid as to form, place, or time. Those people closest to the person who has died should let themselves be led to plan whatever seems to them the most fitting event.

Funerals or memorial services need not be morbid or barbaric or totally painful experiences. When we are unprepared for handling death and the necessary arrangements at mortuaries, only the strangeness and the sorrow may be apparent. But when we have imagined death ahead of time we can act appropriately and responsibly when the time comes.

The funeral can and should be a time of celebration—for the life of the person who has died and for the life we all share. With reverence and respect we say farewell to the body, the earthly remains of the dead. We do not avoid the reality of death. We may mourn because the death seems senseless and too soon, or we may thank God that the dying has brought release from suffering. In both those responses, however, we celebrate the person and affirm our own participation in the rhythm of living and dying.

CONCLUSION OR BEGINNING

For those who see death as "conclusion," this one and only lifetime has great importance. There is no illusion of life after death where we get another chance or where we are judged for missing this one. There is no "pie in the sky by and by" as a reward to justify the sufferings of this life, and no punishment for causing others to suffer. If, in this view, there is no new life to look forward to, there at least are no old self and guilt-problems to drag along. For these people living in death will be seen primarily as living in the memories and deeds of others in this life.

For those who see death as "beginning," the act of dying is but a step along the way from one life to another. The nature of this new life may be seen in various ways according to the different religious views. It may be seen as reincarnation into another body. It may be seen as reunification with the life source itself. It may be seen as an entrance into some form of fellowship with the creator of life.

In the last analysis, of course, we do not know whether death is conclusion or beginning. My own conviction leads me to say it is both. Just as life and death are two sides of the same coin, the figure and ground of the same picture, so also are ends and beginnings. There cannot be one without the other. We came from something, we know not what; we will go to something, we know not what. Perhaps in the achievement of our death we will embrace our conclusion and our beginning in a new wholeness beyond both.

We achieve our death by dying in life. In so doing we may achieve our life by living in death. And who knows the other side of our imaginings? We already sense the presence of others living on in death in our midst. Perhaps that sharing continues when we die.

Not long ago a twenty-five-year-old friend of mine was called home when her mother died suddenly. Her father had died when she was only three, and her mother had lived with a strong sense of her young husband's presence throughout the rest of her life as she raised their daughter. My friend described an astonishing experience she had as she sat with her mother's body in the funeral home. She saw in fantasy her father join her mother in the room. Both of them were young, happy, and laughing. They played, chased each other, then danced out of the mortuary and up into the nearby hills. There they turned and waved to her, took hands, and went running off over the hill.

C. S. Lewis suggests in *Letters to Malcolm* that perhaps there will be a stepping over from this life to a kind of sleep:

Then the new earth and sky, the same yet not the same as these, will rise in us as we have risen in Christ. And once again, after who knows what aeons of the silence and the dark, the birds will sing and the waters flow, and lights and shadows move across the hills, and the faces of our friends laugh upon us with amazed recognition.

Guesses, of course, only guesses. If they are not true, something better will be. For "we know that we shall be made like Him, for we shall see Him as He is." [P. 124]

CONCLUDING REFLECTIONS: THE READINESS IS ALL

. . . there's a special providence in the fall of a sparrow. If it be now, 'tis not to come; if it be not to come, it will be now; if it be not now, yet it will come: the readiness is all.

[*Hamlet,* Act V, Scene II]

Sooner or later, the sparrow falls, the grass withers, you and I die. Ah, me! I wish it were not so. I wish things were different. But if life were different, it is unlikely I would have whatever it is I now wish would never die.

In the first session of a class I attended on "Death and Dying," we were asked to write how we felt about our own death. I wrote the following:

I like living. I like being. I like existing in this world —familiar, known. I don't like the idea of things going on without me. I like to think of people I know and love as always being there. Yet I know I have grown and found greater personal freedom after the death of others—and that may happen for others with mine. But I don't want to think that has to wait for death to happen. I want change and growth and newness now. I'd like to be able to see death as part of that continuum.

158

To find for myself a style of openness where I can trust newness, affirm change, and embrace growth in my living and in my dying—this is at the heart of my own quest as I seek the achievement of my death.

From experience we know the new can only come through the death of the old. Our dying makes room for new lives to grow. Through death we may enter a new realm of living now hidden from view. This kind of dying is part of the rhythm of life and death. It is when we try to live as though dead that we are least human and least true to our created nature. To be dead in feeling or mind, or dead in active involvement is to miss the depth of living as well as the fulfillment of dying.

TIMELY CHOICES

We cannot choose not to die. "If it isn't now, it will come; if it isn't to come, it will be now; if it isn't now, yet it will come." But we *can* make a lot of choices in regard to *how* we die.

You and I can decide how to relate to others about dying and death—both theirs and ours. If you are terminally ill, do you want to be told? Can you talk to others about death, or do you think we should not talk about it? Do you know why you feel the way you do? Would you be able to maintain an ongoing relationship with someone who is dying? Would you want your friends to do the same for you? I realize that we are often capable of doing more when it is required than we thought possible. I am sure this is true of living in dying—with others and with ourselves. But we have a better chance of becoming what we want to be if we imagine and aspire and make choices that help us realize our vision.

We can make out wills to ensure a proper and dignified dispersal of our possessions when we die. We can make known to others our wishes regarding heroic measures to prolong our life. Have you considered whether you want life-sustaining measures to be used indefinitely if there is no hope for your recovery from fatal illness or accident? We can make plans for the care of family members before we die. We can make arrangements about our funeral and especially about our burial. Have you determined where you want to be buried and if you want cremation?

We can make decisions about specific matters of concern that others might not feel competent to decide. For instance, do you want to give your body to a mortuary science college? Do you want to donate any organs that are usable for medical purposes—eyes, heart, liver, kidneys, glands, etc.? One woman with crippling arthritis has willed her hands to a center for research on the disease. For her it is a way she can live on in death and make a contribution to the living. These decisions must be made ahead of time, however, and should be made known to others now, for the donation must be made immediately after death.

We can also make choices about the time we have now: how do we use it, with what do we fill it, why do we live it? It is through the awareness of death that we come to know the value of time and of the present in which we live. For many people the realization that they will die has given them a new sense of the wonder of each day and a contentment to try to live each day fully. The boundary that death represents gives to my time a unique character; *I* must respond to whatever opportunities come to me and thus give shape to the particular experiences that are mine.

Knowing we die we can begin to "sit loose" to all the *things* of this world. Robert Kavanaugh writes perceptively about the need to let go not only of people but of the earthly treasures we've accumulated—possessions that sometimes bind us too tightly to life. "We begin to die well," he suggests, "the first day we learn to cherish the world we know without crippling dependency on it."

PERSONAL STYLE

As mentioned before, we need to become more consciously aware of who we are as persons, of what style best fits us as individuals, and of what view of death is most appropriate to that style.

Each of us has only one death to die, whether that death comes at seventeen or forty-five or ninety. And it is possible, I think, to die that death with style—one's own unique and particular style. Whether it is accepting, defiant, sensual, humorous, tragic, questing, or some combination of these, living that style into one's death can add the flair, the verve, the energy by which death is made one's own. As such, it should be regarded as the crowning achievement of our lives.

I do not know that it is any easier to accept death at the end of a long life than it is at the end of a short one. When Babe Ruth retired with his record 714 home runs he was asked if he had any regrets. He replied, "Sure, I wish I'd hit 715 homers." There is always more we'd like to do. Even people with terminal illness are usually content as long as they can enjoy some little thing each day. It is only when the pain is too great, the weariness of age or illness too heavy that a person will say, "Come, sweet death." Although death at the end of many years seems more "appropriate" than death for the young, it is not always true that a long life is a full and rich one. If life is short, we can still have in depth what we lack in length.

We don't know whether death will come to us early or late—unless we choose suicide. Most of what we've discussed in these pages takes for granted a fairly long life. Such an assumption is proper since advances in the health sciences have greatly increased life expectancy, and we do not know what the future holds.

I often see in young people an attitude that appears to assert, "Nothing can possibly happen to me! My youth and strength are a shield of immortality around me." If they had more awareness of their vulnerability, their fragile humanity, and the real possibility of death, I think they would have more care for themselves and others and less unthinking recklessness. Not that the knowledge of death should keep us from taking risks. It can, however, prompt us to consider our values and priorities: in what ways do I risk my life and for what causes?

For instance, if we seriously imagine how we would like to die, few of us would choose being smashed up in an accident on the highway. While we cannot prevent that from happening, perhaps we can live in ways that will minimize the possibility—driving carefully and at reasonable speeds; not taking meaningless chances with our own lives or the lives of others; not driving while sleepy or drinking.

It is true that we may not die in the way we have imagined or in the specific way we would choose. But perhaps by imagining how we would like to die it will not come in trivial ways or be so scary whenever or however it arrives—like rehearsing for a performance that is the climax of the drama of our own lives. Through imagination we can learn something of the vitality of living and dying from the "divine" Sarah Bernhardt who was struck with her final illness while rehearsing a new play at the age of seventy-eight.

Rousing from a semicoma she asked, "When do I go on?" and died shortly afterward.

IN READINESS

Accidental death is always possible. Even so, what we have been saying about living and dying with style still applies. If we live with style and meet each day with as much fullness of life as we can embody, then dying suddenly will not find us unprepared. Indeed, as Hamlet says, "the readiness is all." Sooner than we might have hoped, yes; different from what we had imagined, yes. But when we have accepted death in life we are, in a sense, always ready.

Such a readiness means neither a gloomy absorption with dying nor a death wish. To live each conscious moment as if it were the very last one would give each parting, each completed sentence, each glance, such a terrible weight that living would be only a burden.

To be ready is to know that we carry in us our complete life—including our death—all the time. At any moment I am my past experience, my present reality, my future aspiration. My death today will be different in degree from the one I will die next year or whenever, but it will be mine, achieved in my own style. I will always have a few more things I would like to do. I, like the King of Siam, have my "etcetera, etcetera, etcetera." Part of being ready is knowing I may have projects cut short, tasks broken off in midstream. Even understanding I may not complete them, however, I still live as though I will.

In Hartford, Connecticut, on May 19, 1780, an event took place known in history as "The Dark Day." A gradual inexplicable darking of the sun—not an eclipse, not caused by fog or cloud—caused the people to believe that the biblical end of the world had finally come. The state legislature was in session on that same day. As the panic outside increased and finally penetrated the legislative hall, many members demanded adjournment. Colonel Abraham Davenport, speaker of the Connecticut House of Representatives, was presiding. As the adjournment clamor grew, he rose and spoke: "The day of judgment is either approaching or it is not. If it is not, there is no cause for adjournment. If it is, I choose to be found doing my duty. I wish, therefore, that candles may be brought." Colonel Davenport knew what it meant to be ready!

While readiness does not mean radical alteration in the way we live, it can impart freedom for living with heightened awareness. Richard Kisonak, after discovering he had less than a year to live, wrote, "I made up my mind to live one day at a time, enjoying life to the fullest, and soon I was doing just that."[1] And Richie Cope, given a second life through a heart transplant, observed,

I smell the grass when I cut it. . . . I hear the song of a bird. I watch a cloud go by, hear the cry of a gull and watch the waves, and nobody can set a price on that. I never saw them until life was about to be snatched away and it was given back to me. My life was a flat plane before. Now it's three-dimensional.[2]

Even those who know they will die soon may be surprised. In a group of cancer patients interviewed concerning their feelings about their terminal illness, two who mentioned they might be killed in accidents did in fact die accidentally. And for some, a "terminal" illness surprises them by not being terminal.

[1] "Only One Year to Live," *International Herald Tribune,* April 28, 1972.

[2] Quoted by Bob Keeler, Newsday Service, "Spending His Borrowed Time," *San Francisco Sunday Examiner and Chronicle,* March 19, 1972.

Preparation for readiness should begin in childhood. There are many occasions when questions will arise naturally: when pets die, or friends or relatives or public figures. Children usually respond at their own rate to the honest feelings of others. To try to shield them from experiences of death not only denies them contact with a natural reality of life, but cuts them off from participation in a deep emotional event with the family. By sharing with the young our own interpretations of death we help build their resources for seeing death as part of life.

It is never easy to accept one's own death, but if children experience death in a loving, sharing context with others it can be less fearful. Some people suggest death education in the schools as valid and necessary preparation. Certainly, death fears that are repressed in early life have a way of reasserting themselves in other ways later: insomnia, schizophrenia, paranoia about separation. It would be healthy to have a context in which children could talk naturally about their feelings and be exposed to the various cultural resources and religious interpretations to aid them in their understanding of death.

Death will come. The challenge is whether we will be ready to achieve it when it arrives.

BEING *AND* NOT BEING

Why humans should be born and die is one of many mysteries confronting us. It is reported that as Gertrude Stein lay dying she said to her friend Alice B. Toklas, "What is the answer?" When there was only silence, Gertrude Stein smiled and said, "In that case, what is the question?" The search for meaning is never-ending. Perhaps it is revealed only *in* our living and dying. Rainer Maria Rilke wrote to his friend:

. . . to be patient toward all that is unsolved in your heart and to try to love the questions *themselves* like locked rooms and like books that are written in a very foreign tongue. Do not now seek the answers, which cannot be given you because you would not be able to live them. And the point is, to live everything. *Live* the questions now. Perhaps you will then gradually, without noticing it, live along some distant day into the answer. [*Letters to a Young Poet,* trans. M. D. Herder Norton (New York: W. W. Norton, 1934), p. 35]

In the last analysis, it is not the question "to be or not to be?" but rather the affirmation "to be *and* not to be." It is not a matter of living *or* dying, but of living *and* dying. It is possible to live with simultaneous images of people, places, feelings, states of being. Life is not a big either/or. We die in life, we live in death. We can be ready even though never completely ready. We can love life and living, yet let go into death since that too is part of the life we love. My sister said to me not long ago, "How can we finally be afraid of death and not want to die when so many people we love are already there waiting for us?" In our commitment to all of life and in continuity with those we love, we already know what it is to be and not to be at the same time.

In religious thought the word "eschatology" refers to the doctrine of "last things." Recognizing the finitude of human existence this becomes a way of anticipating what may happen when human time and history come to an end. The eschaton is often described as the fulfillment of all things, the end of time when humanity is judged for what has and hasn't been done.

In my own thinking I do not know if there is an eschaton for all creation or not. But I do think we are always living in terms of "last things." Always within us there are things dying and others being born. Always we are ending some activities and beginning others. In every moment we are judged for what we have and haven't done. At any instant my own time may be fulfilled and come to an end.

We are always living toward the eschaton, toward fulfillment. And even now we can, through our living imagination, enter into our death and roam around exploring. When we come back from that mysterious country we may decide to live differently, with greater awareness, in order to achieve that death we have envisioned.

ACHIEVING LIFE AND DEATH

So it goes, back and forth, living and dying, each affecting the other. And it would seem that the achievement of death is not really distinguishable from the achievement of life.

It is in the interaction of the two that we discover our selves. On one of the fantasy trips I took a few years ago, we were directed to go in imagination into a cave where we would find a very old and wise person sitting by a fire. We were then instructed to approach this sage and ask a question. I did so, asking, "What does it mean?" (That's a good one, I thought to myself!) Then we were told to have the person speak and answer the question. Almost without hesitation my wise old one (in my own mind) said, "It *is* what it means." Having gotten such a prompt response I took advantage of my fantasy trip to ask another question, "Who am I?" And back came the answer, "You are who you are *becoming.*"

I would never have believed it. To find within the fantasy recesses of my own imagination answers to two such puzzling questions. Granted, the answers are a bit elliptical, but how could they not be? And those answers have served me well in subsequent years. We can both become what we are and be what we are becoming. Life and death *are,* and that is what they mean.

It is all mystery, our living and our dying. Not long before he died Mark Pelgrin wrote of his experience looking at a Chinese mandala:

> The dark malignant powers that seemed to have beset me are not malignant as long as I stare at the mandala and say over and over, "all is well," put your trust in unknown, far larger elements than you can ever be completely aware of. The centre is a square, and within, a circle, and within, a curious circular dot, but that is all you write down. The centre is a *tremendum* and a radiant mystery. [*And a Time to Die,* p. 156]

As we achieve our life and death in that sense of mystery, it becomes finally a question of whether we can trust death as we trust life—as we trust loving, being loyal, being faithful, planting seeds, waiting for spring, going to sleep each night. Being able to trust is what we call "grace." I'm not sure how it comes, but mostly we have to desire it and be ready to receive it when it is present.

Perhaps it is by trust that I can achieve my death. To be aware of myself—my feelings, my beliefs, my aspirations—and trust that self. To discover a style that expresses my self in the best way and trust that style. To explore the implications of my style of living for the way I want to achieve my death and trust the changes that may ensue. To be able finally to integrate my view of death and my view of life and live in the reality of both. This, it seems to me, is a central task of living that offers a glorious possibility—to live in trust, to make choices that include my dying, to experience that final creative surge. I can achieve my death. I can live and die—with style!

FURTHER READING

Individual Perspectives and Interpretations

Hendin, David. *Death as a Fact of Life*. New York: W. W. Norton & Co., 1973.

Hinton, John. *Dying*. Baltimore: Penguin Books, 1967.

Hocking, William Ernest. *The Meaning of Immortality in Human Experience*. New York: Harper & Brothers, 1957.

Kavanaugh, Robert E. *Facing Death*. Los Angeles: Nash Publishing, 1972.

Kübler-Ross, Elisabeth. *On Death and Dying*. New York: The Macmillan Co., 1970.

Lepp, Ignace. *Death and Its Mysteries*. Trans. Bernard Murchland. New York: The Macmillan Co., 1968.

Mannes, Marya. *Last Rights: A Case for the Good Death*. New York: William Morrow & Co., 1974.

Miller, Randolph Crump. *Live Until You Die*. Philadelphia: Pilgrim Press, 1973.

Neale, Robert E. *The Art of Dying*. New York: Harper & Row, 1973.

White, Hugh Vernon. "Life, Death and Eternal Life," chapter 12, *Truth and Person in Christian Theology*. New York: Oxford University Press, 1963.

Personal Encounters and Experiences

Alsop, Stewart. *Stay of Execution: A Sort of Memoir*. New York: J. B. Lippincott Co., 1973.

Gollwitzer, Helmut; Kuhn, Käthe; and Schneider, Reinhold, eds. *Dying We Live*. Trans. Reinhard C. Kuhn. New York: The Seabury Press, 1968.

Gunther, John. *Death Be Not Proud*. New York: Harper & Brothers, 1949.

Lewis, C. S. *A Grief Observed*. New York: The Seabury Press, 1963.

Pelgrin, Mark. *And a Time to Die*. Ed. Dr. Sheila Moon and Dr. Elizabeth B. Howes. Sausalito, Calif.: Contact Editions, 1962.

Stringfellow, William. *A Second Birthday*. Garden City, N. Y.: Doubleday & Co., 1970.

Wertenbaker, Lael Tucker. *Death of a Man*. New York: Random House, 1957.

General Surveys and Symposia

Choron, Jacques. *Death and Modern Man*. New York: The Macmillan Co., 1972.

————. *Death and Western Thought*. New York: Collier Books, 1963.

Cousins, Ewert H., ed. *Hope and the Future of Man*. Philadelphia: Fortress Press, 1972.

Dumont, Richard G., and Foss, Dennis C. *The American View of Death: Acceptance or Denial?* Cambridge, Mass.: Schenkman Publishing Co., 1972.

Feifel, Herman, ed. *The Meaning of Death*. New York: McGraw-Hill Book Co., 1959.

Fulton, Robert, ed. *Death and Identity*. New York: John Wiley & Sons, 1965.

Green, Betty R., and Irish, Donald P., eds. *Death Education: Preparation for Living*. Cambridge, Mass.: Schenkman Publishing Co., 1971.

Mills, Liston O., ed. *Perspectives on Death*. Nashville: Abingdon Press, 1969.

Scott, Nathan A., Jr., ed. *The Modern Vision of Death*. Richmond: John Knox Press, 1967.

Toynbee, Arnold and others. *Man's Concern With Death*. New York: McGraw-Hill Book Co., 1969.

INDEX

172

174